He'll Never Amount To Anything
A Farm Boy's Stories

Wayne Feder

Copyright © 2015 by Wayne Feder

All rights reserved. This book or any portion thereof may not be reproduced or used in any manner whatsoever without the express written permission of the publisher except for the use of brief quotations in a book review or scholarly journal.

ISBN 978-1511889285

Introduction

I dedicate these stories to my father, Ervin Feder. Dad was born in 1898, the fifth son of a hardworking pioneer family. He quit school in sixth grade to work full-time on the farm with his parents and three brothers, eventually becoming a highly successful farmer. Dad worked hard six days a week, did what had to be done when it needed to be done, and hung up his clothes when he took them off at night.

I fooled around. I played sports and games. I hung out at the pool hall and played pinball in the Noonan Hotel lobby. At school I ignored or haphazardly completed my assignments and read library books instead of paying attention in class. At home I did the work I needed to do but never accepted responsibility as I should have and as was expected of me. I know I greatly disappointed Dad when I told him I wanted to attend college instead of staying on the farm.

Like Peter Pan, I guess I didn't want to grow up. My favorite children's story is "How Tom Beat Captain Najork and His Hired Sportsmen," a tale of how Tom, using all the things he learned while "fooling around," was able to defeat his old nemesis.

I am now an amateur genealogist. Our family history folder at the Watonwan County Historical Society in my hometown of Madelia, Minnesota, includes a short family history written by an unknown author. In it, my Uncle Ed is quoted as saying, in reference to me, "He'll never amount to anything." I certainly can't argue with my uncle's assessment, based as it was on his observations and most likely on discussions with other members of my family and our community.

It takes a long time to grow up. Some of us take longer than others. Let's just say my childhood was sufficiently long to accumulate a large storehouse of memories. I make no pretense as a writer, but do present these stories as being honestly represented and accurately told, at least so far as I can recall. From time to time you may run across someone who claims to have been present at one or more of the events that follow and refutes the accuracy of their telling. To them I say: "Go write your own stories."

Acknowledgements

I am amazed and thankful that my parents, Ervin and Hilda, gave me the freedom and trust, sometimes misguided, to carry out my adventures.

My wife Lynda, my children Casey, Cody, and Darcy, and my sons-in-law Jim and Ben have been forced to endure my time-consuming pastime, tolerating me as I ignore them to hog the computer and hunch over my keyboard.

Darcy has been a great help in critiquing, arranging, and proofing my stories.

Without Casey's proofreading, organizing, and editing, this book would never have been published.

My friend Chris encourages me in my writing and attempts, without much success, to teach me the rudiments of grammar.

Thanks all.

Table of Contents

World War II	1
Eye Drops	2
Barn Fire	3
Peat	4
Cars	5
Tonsils	7
A Wagonload of Sand	8
Touching the Pig	10
Crack the Whip	12
The Nickel	15
The Lone Ranger	16
Crime and Punishment	17
The Visitation	19
The Haymow	20
Lumberyard	22
The Cart	24
Bubblegum	25
Horse	26
An Unfortunate Event	27
Threshing	28
The Kettle in Underwear	30
Snow Day	31
Tiling	32
Herb	34
Gang War	36
Taboo	37
Frank and Florence	38
The Book Report	42
Snowball Fight	44
Tackle Tag	45
Wilson's Woods	47
The Joke	50
Swimming Lessons	52
First Hunt	53
Unlikely Hero	55
Duck Hunting	56
Workup	58
The Playground	60
The Bully	63
Rafts	64
Snow	68
Croquet	71
The Roller Rink	74
Marbles	76
Taken For a Ride	78
State Fair	80
Saturday Night	84
Trapping	89
Football	92
Monkey Bars	93
Mistaken Identity	95
The Incident	96
A Short Vacation	97
The Ball Game	99
Whitetail	100
Ice Fishing	101
Climbing	103
Dogs	109
The Philosopher	114
The Crush	115
Field and Stream	116
Cattle	118
Magical Morning	128
Ice Sledding	130
Impeach Earl Warren	131
A Lesson in Speed	133
Swans	134
A Cat and a Brother	135
Fishing	137
Lloyd's Barn	139
Opening Day	141
Running Underwater	142
Krajewski For President	143
Roadboarding	145
Wally	146
Accident	147
A Brush With Stardom	148
Alfred E. Newman	150
The Nun	151
Sputnik	154

Table of Contents

Grand Canyon	155	Cultivating	174
What I Learned in School	158	Heart Attack	177
Bulldozers	162	Vern's	178
Jackrabbits	163	New Year's Eve	184
Running	164	Birds	185
Water Skiing	169	Fooling Around	188
Ice Cream Cone	171	4-H	190
The Cannon	173	Picking Corn	198

WORLD WAR II

"The Klinkner kids are coming," I shouted, rushing into the kitchen where Mom was working at the sink. The Klinkner family did in fact have more than a dozen children, but the slowly approaching horde turned out to not be our neighbors to the north but a group of total strangers. The militia.

Mother and I stood at the bottom of our driveway and watched a double row of pseudo-soldiers march past our farm, each with a wooden rifle on his shoulder. They were a motley crew of mixed-aged men dressed in civilian clothes, all definitely marching to the beat of their own drummers. To add to their decidedly unmilitary bearing, many turned to grin at a small boy as they passed.

I assume I was watching some kind of home guard, training to protect our community from the dreaded Huns or Asian hordes. It was the closest this four-year-old came to serving his country during World War II.

Small squares of waxed paper covered our kitchen counter. On each was a white mound of homemade divinity or a piece of dark fudge. Mother waved her spatula in my direction. "Don't you dare touch." I didn't touch and I didn't taste; the candy was spoken for. Each piece was carefully wrapped in its paper, divided into two equal piles, and painstakingly packed in sturdy cardboard boxes. The candy was for my cousins, Russell and William, each serving somewhere in the Pacific. Sugar was strictly rationed and not to be wasted on selfish young boys.

The sky began to fill with airplanes. Soon they were everywhere, planes of all sizes and all shapes, singly and in loose formation, swooping and diving above our farm. Then they were gone. The drill I witnessed must have originated from the airfields in Minneapolis and St. Paul.

I was playing in our front lawn one warm summer evening when suddenly a car, windows rolled down, raced into our yard, partially obscured by an accompanying cloud of dust. Dad's cousin Lloyd Biisser, at the wheel, hollered as he came. Dad rushed to the car from the barn and Mom from the house. Smiling from ear to ear my mother did a small dance, turned, and yelled to me across the lawn, "The war is over."

Eye Drops

I was four years old when I developed pink eye in my left eye. A visit to Doctor Grimes' office and a quick stop at Bill's Drugstore had us heading home with the proper treatment. It was nothing a few eye drops wouldn't cure.

The bottle of medicine came out, and a menacing dropper waved in front of me. I had a fit. I threw a tantrum and screamed and cried. Finally, as a last resort before holding me down and administering the liquid, Dad decided to use reason and demonstrate how simple the procedure was. Standing, he tilted his head back and let a drop fall into the bottom of his eye.

A strange look crossed his face. He rushed to the sink, stuck his head under the faucet and began flushing his eye with running water. Soon an ugly red mark appeared across the lower part of his eye below the pupil, one that lasted for many weeks.

The drugstore had allowed an unlicensed intern to fill my prescription. A caustic chemical had been sent home instead of the prescribed drug.

I remember Dad telling me about the incident when I was older. He said they were prepared to hold me down and put drops in both of my eyes to make sure the problem didn't spread. I would have been blind.

Those were the days before lawsuits. A few weeks later, our family received a set of sterling silverware as a gift, a set Lynda and I still have today.

Barn Fire

I never knew Doc Dahl, but I think he was a veterinarian. One morning when I was about five years old, Dad informed me that Doc had had a barn fire and that he was going to look at the results. I'm sure I begged to go along. In any case I ended up in the car and off we went. Doc's farm was six miles straight north of our farm but had to be reached by a roundabout way because the roads didn't go straight through.

The barn was mostly gone, just piles of charcoal, partially burned timbers, and smoldering hay. The livestock wasn't mostly gone; it was just half gone. Charred cows with their necks still in stanchions stretched the length of the barn. Closer to the end where we stood, four large work horses lay in their former stalls; much of their bodies had burned away. The large masses of their rumps were their most fire-resistant parts. The smell of singed hair and burned flesh mingled with that of the still-smoking barn.

Barn fires were hard for a young boy to forget.

PEAT

Adults in my sphere began talking about the big peat fire in Herman Anderson's drained lakebed. It was early winter, and fresh snow covered the ground. We decided to check it out.

The peat, actually soil formed long ago from decayed marsh vegetation, had been burning for several weeks. I have since learned that many attempts had been made to put out the smoldering fire with no success. What attracted the crowds to the scene that day was the fresh snow cover.

We walked to the bank that overlooked the lake bottom and were treated to a surreal scene. As far as we could see, patches of smoke were billowing through the snow. What kind of world was this where the earth could burn? I now think that the melting snow was adding steam to the smoke, greatly magnifying nature's performance.

What foolish parents I had. We returned home and continued on with our lives as if nothing terrible was happening. I was put to bed as usual. How long would it take for the fire to spread underground the three miles to our house? I know I was surprised the following morning, and for several mornings after, that our farm was still standing.

CARS

My mom bought eggs from Mrs. Klinkner. One summer morning, when I was four and Marlys seven, Mom parked our old pre-war Ford sedan in front of the Klinkner house and went in to make her weekly purchase.

A short time after she entered the house, the car began to roll, slowly at first, then faster as the incline steepened. Fifty yards down the hill were the likely targets: a barn, an old apple tree, and a netting fence surrounding the cattle yard.

Marlys' adrenaline-induced plan was simple. Jump.

In an instant I was pulled and pushed out the rolled-down backseat window, closely followed by my sister.

The car chose the apple tree.

Cars were made of better stuff in those days; a dent in the front bumper was its only disfigurement.

I don't know if I learned any lessons from the experience, but I suppose my mother learned to put the car in gear before shutting it off.

Dad installed a newfangled compass on the dashboard of his car. One afternoon he was driving us home from school when, as we reached the west end of Main Street, a short in the wiring system caused the light in the compass to begin sparking and smoking. Dad's first reaction was to slow the car and move toward the curb. Mine was more dramatic. In an instant I clawed my way over my sister, yanked open the door, and jumped.

When your feet first touch the ground after you have jumped from a moving car, it feels as if the street is moving rapidly away from you. The sensation is soon forgotten as you begin sliding along the concrete.

A few contusions and a ruined shirt later, I climbed back into the car and we continued our journey. Dad suggested I might have overreacted.

Madelia was mostly shut down on Sunday mornings. Marlys and I usually walked the two blocks from Sunday school and waited for our ride home in the lobby of the post office.

One Sunday morning, I raced up from the church trying to keep up with my Cousin David. He dashed across Main Street from between two parked cars, and I blindly followed.

George Latourell drove a light gray coupe. The car struck me near its passenger side headlight. I remember the impact and waking up next to the curb with George and a small group of people staring down at me. Amateur examiners determined that my limbs moved properly, and, in spite of a large bump on the back of my head, I was acceptably healthy.

For the next several years I gave George and his gray car a wide berth whenever I saw them approaching.

TONSILS

The remedy for nearly every childhood ailment was the same: the tonsils had to come out. Mine were extracted when I was five.

I wasn't sure what tonsils were, but I was angry. We got up early, in the dark, and I was informed I would not be allowed to eat breakfast. Mom and Dad were upstairs dressing. I defiantly pulled up a chair, climbed on the kitchen counter, and opened the cupboard, eyeing the row of cereal boxes. The command had been gravely given. I closed the door and climbed back to the floor.

A wire mesh cone was placed over my mouth and nose, and I was instructed to count to ten. A circle of white masks stared down, watching as an ether-infused cloth was draped over the wire.

I spent a day recuperating at my Cousin Tommy's house in North Mankato. Dad had taken the car to do chores, so the following morning Tommy and his mother brought us home.

In spite of the difficulty swallowing, I was anxious to show off my new teeter-totter. Tommy, slightly heavier, paused, holding me at the top. Then he jumped. My end crashed to the ground.

We ran for the house, Tommy in fear, and me crying, dripping red.

A Wagonload Of Sand

In the forties, summers were hot and endless. I was five or six years old. My mom's best friend, Catherine Sorenson, was visiting for the afternoon; her son Jimmy and I wandered the farm looking for adventure. For a while we watched my dad as he unloaded hay from one of several large hayracks lined up in the yard. For some reason he was working alone, which made the job more tedious than usual. Dad would climb up on the load of slippery hay and fasten the ends of the top sling to a hook on the inch-thick hay rope. He then climbed down and walked to the backside of the barn where the big work team stood patiently waiting. The team, rigged to the far end of the hay rope, were driven along the side of the barn, lifting the twisting, creaking sling with its hundreds of pounds of hay upward toward the projecting peak of the barn. The sounds abruptly changed, and a puff of chaff flew as the hay reached its pinnacle, made a ninety-degree turn, and rode the wheeled hay carrier along its track and into the black cavern of the barn.

When the hay was as far into the barn as he wanted, Dad would back up the team and return to the hayrack. He picked up a long, thin trip rope that was attached to the carrier and gave it a sharp pull, releasing one end of the sling and dropping the hay into the haymow. He then pulled the carrier back to the peak and the rope and empty sling down to the wagon. The sling ropes from the next bundle were hooked to the big rope and the process repeated until all five or six bundles were deposited into the haymow. Haying was not a new experience; we soon lost interest and moved on with our day.

Water is like a magnet to young boys, and we soon wandered through the pasture to the large slough a few hundred yards east of our farm site. The slough had a mud bottom and corresponding mud shoreline. For some reason, one area of the shore was coated with a dusting of sand, which to our imagination became a treasure to be mined and used to fill a new sandbox. We returned to the farm and picked up the tools of our trade: my Radio Flyer wagon and a couple of small pails.

Mining is time consuming. We hauled the wagon to the project, dug and sloshed around in the work area, and slowly filled our wagon with our quartz-like treasure.

We staggered under our burden, pushing and pulling our load of muddy sand across the rough pasture and up the seemingly steep hill to our farm. The scene that unfolded as we approached the farmyard will forever remain imprinted in my mind. I can see everything in slow motion. In the distance Mother and Catherine seem to freeze for a fraction of a second. Suddenly all becomes frenzy. They are screaming and pointing as Catherine runs toward us, and Mom, skirt flying, turns and runs as fast as she can toward the barn.

I don't know how long we had been gone and I have no memories of any events that followed, but today, in my mind's eye, I can see everything as it unfolded. Jimmy and I are missing. The search gets more and more frantic until the only place left to look is the hayloft. There is hollering to see if we can be heard. Dad, sweating in the heat and dust, digs franticly, attempting to move the tons of freshly dropped hay. There are thoughts of suffocation and of sharp pitchforks. Mother rushing into the barn shouting, "We found them." I don't remember ever hearing about the incident again. I can imagine it was too frightening to think or talk about. I hope there was no placing of blame or guilt.

The sandbox was never built.

Jimmy, on the right, and me, at the Sorenson farm.

Touching The Pig

I like this story because of its catchy title. Ours was a cattle farm. Dad made his living buying cattle in the fall, feeding them the corn we raised on our farm, and selling them a year later at the stockyards in South St. Paul. However, there had been a time when beef was not the primary source of income on our farm.

The cow stanchions and the pipe calf and bullpens in our little barn were the only reminder of Dad's purebred dairy herd, condemned and destroyed in the thirties after an outbreak of brucellosis. Pigs replaced the cows. They were farrowed and fed in our big brick barn. This barn, built in the late thirties, was completely destroyed during a major tornado in 1939. A new barn arose, phoenix-like, on the foundation of the old. This new building housed pigs and large flocks of ewes. Dad lambed the sheep in groups of fifty, with the birthing spread over several weeks to even out the workload.

My sister Marlys holding a lamb.
The sheep are in a protected pen between our two barns.

Sheep disappeared just before the dawn of my memory; my only connection with them was the pile of wooden lambing gates stacked along the north haymow wall. Each ewe and her newborn lambs were isolated in small pens for a few days to make sure they bonded and gained strength before joining the larger flock.

I know you must be waiting for the pigs. I have one memory of this species; all our hogs must have been sold from the farm by the mid-forties. Woven wire fences, designed to keep hogs or sheep from escaping, enclosed our fields. In the fall, after the corn was picked, animals were turned loose to forage on the leaves and fallen ears.

Two hundred yards north of our farm, a large cement culvert passed under our gravel road, built to allow animals free movement from one side to the other. A narrow fenced alley led from our farm to the culvert.

Pigs are smart but stubborn. On this particular day, Dad had herded some big sows down the alley and had them corralled at the mouth of the culvert. They had decided they were perfectly happy to stay on our side of the road. Dad knew better than to try to push or bully a four-hundred-pound pig; he resorted to guile and trickery. A big sow, her body halfway in, stared west through the culvert. Dad, on the west side, looked back. He called, "Sooey! Sooey!" He threw corn in front of the pig, and he coaxed and cajoled. He was getting angry and frustrated.

Dad needed help. He gave me a thin stick. "When I tell you, touch her lightly on the back. Remember, just a little." He disappeared across the road, obviously prepared to perform some kind of magic. "Now." I sprawled on my stomach above the culvert, stretched out the stick, and touched her wiry back. She grunted. Dad began scurrying back and forth, issuing new instructions with each trip.

We took one last look at her protruding half and, defeated, walked home together.

Crack The Whip

My skating fortunes were dictated by the weather, wind being the most important factor. A strong wind in early winter, when the ice was freezing, would result in a cut and ridged surface, ruining an entire skating season. Lighter winds at freeze-up made for rough, but tolerable, skating. Some years cold weather arrived during a snowstorm and the surface didn't actually become ice, but turned to a grainy pudding, totally unfit for its intended purpose. Occasionally the weather was perfect: the temperatures would drop on a quiet clear night and dawn would reveal a spectacular sheet of glass.

I still wasn't home free. Strong winds might arrive in the next day or two, breaking up the fragile ice and leaving a jagged wasteland in its wake. If my luck held, it was time to test the new ice, never mind waiting until it was safe to do so. You could always stay close to shore. If you fell through, what was the harm in that?

Did you ever skate on "rubber ice?" Ice at a critical thickness and temperature will bend, radiating little cracks from the point of stress. The trick to navigating ice of this type is to maintain your speed, never slowing until your runners have safely returned to solid ground.

Even in the best years, perfect conditions were fleeting; the snow would surely come. It sometimes arrived soft and fluffy. Wearing five-buckle boots, or your skates if it was not too deep, snow of this type was easily shoveled. Blizzards were the worst; fine particles of snow were blown into rows of hard immovable drifts. The season was over.

Many of my skating memories revolve around frozen toes. I was doubly cursed. Poor circulation kept my feet cold even in my warmest boots. What chance did they have beneath the thin leather of ice skates? My second problem was that I was always a year behind, never thinking of trading in last year's skates until it was too late. This year's feet were squeezed into last year's skates, decreasing my circulation even more.

I became a decent skater, but never as good as my town friends with their regular access to smooth ice and cozy warming houses. The town rink seemed to move from year to year. Several years it was located on the north side of our school playground. I skated there as often as I could talk my mom into driving me to town.

The rink that had the most impact on my childhood was one located across the street from my grandma's house, where the turkey plant was later built.

I was in lower elementary school and had recently graduated from double runner skates to real single bladers. The floodlights were on across the street, and kids of all ages and sizes were circling the rink in a counter-clockwise direction. I walked along the edge of the ice, up the single wooden step, and into the warming house. A large pot-bellied stove at the far end filled the room with heat and the acrid smell of wood smoke. Wooden benches were attached to three walls; under each, scattered in various states of disorder, were pairs of shoes and boots, socks, and an occasional single woolen mitten.

The floor caught and held my attention; I had never seen anything like it. It was wood, but it wasn't. Years of runners had shredded the boards, forming a wooly substance that was beyond identification. Deep paths had been carved into the areas most traveled.

I put on my new skates, shoved my shoes under the bench, and tentatively walked down the step and onto the ice. It took a while to adjust to the single blades, but eventually I was circling with the experts.

I noticed something a little different was happening; some of the big kids were beginning to hold hands and form an ever-longer chain of skaters. As they swept past, the last in line grabbed my hand. "Come on, we're going to crack the whip." Bewildered but game, I skated, or, more accurately, was drug along at an ever-increasing speed.

I now know how crack the whip is played. Once top speed is attained, the lead skater makes a sharp turn and the trailing skaters are spread behind in a wide arc; the farther a skater is from the leader, the faster he moves. The goal of the leader is to apply enough centrifugal force so that at some point, hands unclasp, the chain breaks, and those beyond the break are sent skidding across the ice in a hilarious pileup.

We flew along. Suddenly the sadistic leader made a sharp left; the skaters, following the rules of science, accelerated around the turn, each holding on for dear life. The feet of the end skater were now completely off the ice. As his body approached the horizontal, he lost his grip.

I don't remember sailing through the air and I don't remember landing. I just remember lying on the ice with a ring of faces staring down at me. I couldn't talk or breathe; only the look of panic on my face revealed my condition. Mulligan Osborne, one of the big kids, recognized the symptoms. He grabbed the blades of my skates and began pumping my knees back and forth; perhaps this was a time-honored method of restoring breathing. In this case it only caused more discomfort.

I changed back into my shoes and crossed the street to my grandmother's house.

The Nickel

I attempted to compile a list of all the kids who had ever been in our class as a fun project for my 2008 fiftieth reunion. A few of my classmates were able to add to my list, but none were able to recall Henry. I suppose this shouldn't seem too strange; first grade was a long time ago, and he may not have been with us for the entire year.

Hired men, and those who rented farms, changed addresses frequently, often physically moving their families on March first, "moving day." This was a day of musical chairs, when all movers left their houses in the morning and arrived at their new home that afternoon. We often experienced additions and subtractions to our class the first few days of March. Henry may have stepped off this agricultural merry-go-round and joined us for the last few months of the year.

One cold, late spring day, several of us came upon Henry, sobbing as he wandered around on the soggy, snow-patched lawn in front of our school. I had little knowledge of socioeconomics. Henry wore an old, faded brown, full-length coat. His hair was matted and his nose snotty. He had lost a nickel.

We spread out, scouring the ground. Suddenly a girl in our group straightened up, an Indian Head nickel between her thumb and forefinger.

"How do I know this is your nickel?"

"I know it is."

"If you can tell me what year it is you can have it."

Henry knew.

"I still don't think it's yours."

She pocketed the coin.

At least one of those present understood what had just happened was wrong in so many ways, but lacked the courage and confidence to speak.

The small group slowly drifted away, leaving Henry crying in the mud.

The Lone Ranger

Second graders have a general idea of how tools are used but a greatly inflated perception of their ability to use them. Tools were needed, of course, and were accordingly smuggled to school. How else to gain access to the cabin?

It had been generally known for some time that the Lone Ranger was living in, or was at least frequenting, the old log cabin in the park. He kept the door locked with an old rusty padlock and the windows screened and smeared with dirt to thwart prying eyes. It was imperative that we investigate.

James McCarthy brought a hammer, someone else a saw, and others strange equipment perfectly unsuitable for the task. The first noon we were unsuccessful in gaining access. Undaunted, we hid our tools in anticipation of tomorrow's certain success.

The following morning a messenger arrived at our classroom door. Richard Ellingsberg and Virgil Boelter were summoned to report to Miss McCarthy's room.

We had all heard threats of being sent to the principal's room, but it was a fate no one in our class had actually experienced. Richard and Virgil returned to class after what seemed an eternity. Hushed and awed, all eyes followed them to their seats. The few of us who knew their offense waited for the certain chain reaction to follow. Nothing happened. Virgil and Richard had taken the fall. The rest of our gang never knew in what manner this had been achieved, as the topic never came up for discussion.

Someone had obviously ratted on us. To this day I suspect it was the Lone Ranger.

Crime And Punishment

It was the third or fourth grade when I went bad. The Madelia school system had a wonderful noon schedule: everyone had one hour for lunch with no restrictions placed on leaving the school grounds. The normal situation was to eat lunch as fast as possible, then rush to the playground to play football, tackle-tag, softball, or whatever activity was in season. The large brass school bell would ring when it was five minutes before class was scheduled to begin.

Winter stopped our normal outdoor activities, so we usually walked the two blocks to the Main Street area and wandered through the local stores. Always on the lookout for excitement, Dick Blue and I turned to shoplifting; nothing major, a pencil here or a pack of cigarettes there. Ballpoint pens were a new invention and highly coveted. One evening just before supper I got a call from Dick. He had made a score on his own and would have a new pen for me the next morning at school.

Mom: "Who was that?"

Me: "Dick."

Mom: "What did he want?"

Me: "Nothing."

Mom: "I think it was something."

Ever justifiably suspicious, and probably able to read my guilty face like an open book, Mother tried but failed to uncover my latest activity.

One noon, just before Easter, we hit Ad Broullette's Variety Store. Ad was an excellent marketer; her first words to any prospective customer in my age group were, "How much money do you have?" On this particular day we had a plan: Dick would lure Ad to the back of the store to inquire about some new toy and I would make the heist.

I was faced with a dilemma. Should I go for the candy bars or the large, unwrapped candy Easter eggs stacked in a large pyramid on the counter? The eggs won out. At first, things went well and I quickly ferreted several into my pockets. Suddenly disaster struck in the form of a small but noisy egg avalanche, which quickly brought Ad rushing to the scene. I had been caught sticky-handed. None of the participants in this little tragedy had the slightest doubt as to what was going down; certainly this was not Ad's first rodeo. Her immediate reaction was to get her merchandise back, demanding I empty my pockets. Red-faced and shaky-kneed, I dug out a handful of eggs from each front pocket. "Is that all?" Defiantly I responded, "Search me!"

Ad had the upper hand and now dealt the coup de grace: "Do you think your dad would like to hear about this?" Shamed and stunned, Dick and I slumped out to the sidewalk and headed back toward school. My voice and hand shook as I, with feigned casualness, pulled the remaining eggs from my pockets. For some reason they had lost their sweetness. Luckily the dreaded phone call never materialized, but Ad's desired results had been achieved.

The crime spree was ended.

The Visitation

It was great to have an hour at noon. We could hurry through our hot lunch and still have forty minutes of freedom, the options limited only by our imagination. The seasonal sports and playground activities were popular choices, but sometimes you just had to get away. You could check out the stockyards, sneak into the lumberyard, or wander the back alleys. A store a few blocks to the east even sold rare Frank Buck "Bring Them Back Alive" bubblegum packets.

Main Street, of course, was the most alluring destination. Zimmerman's Five and Ten and Ad's Variety held a seemingly unlimited supply of candy and stocked the newest crazes we couldn't live without. We would stop in the hotel lobby and watch the older boys play pinball, fascinated at how they slowed the ball down by sliding the tips of their shoes under the rear legs of the machine. There were grocery aisles that needed wandering and comic books to be perused. At the last minute we would hurry back to school, just making it to our room before the last bell.

One noon, I may have been in third grade, a friend and I decided to return to school a little early. Nearing the school, we saw that something interesting was happening across the street at the Presbyterian Church. A big black hearse was parked in front, and somber people in dark clothing were filing up the steps and through the big doors. Someone must have died. A quick discussion revealed neither of us had ever seen a dead person. We got in line and moved slowly down the aisle, an organ accompanying our steps. We watched those ahead of us as they quietly paused in front of the open casket, evidently paying their last respects. We did the same. After a reverent look at the definitely dead man, instead of taking a seat with the other mourners, we walked slowly up the aisle, down the steps, and back to school.

The Haymow

The stairway to the haymow of our big cattle barn was an unfriendly place, reached by passing through our herd of whiteface steers and walking through their accumulated manure. We usually played in the little barn.

Little was a relative term. This barn had originally housed Dad's dairy herd and now held his team of workhorses.

The ladder to the haymow was at the end of a long central alley. On the right, Dad's big team of blaze-faced Belgiums nickered and stomped as we passed in front of their manger; on the left, a long row of abandoned rusty cow stanchions and cast iron drinking cups stretched the length of the barn.

I couldn't get into the loft by myself. I could get up the ladder and claw onto the edge of the floor, but the next rung, against the end wall of the barn, was out of my reach. I was stranded. Marlys would go ahead, take my arm, and drag me over the threshold.

Dust danced in the thin beams that streamed through small holes in the roof. Pigeons cooed in the tin cupola or flew overhead and landed on the hay rope at the far end. The haymow smelled of dust, mold, pigeon droppings, and horse.

Mounds of loose hay, feed for the horses, filled the loft in summer but gradually disappeared throughout the long winter and spring. We climbed the slippery hay along its lowest gradient and slid down the steepest slopes.

A large wooden oats bin spanned the front of the barn. It could be accessed from the top of the hay when the barn was full or from a one-by-four ladder on the hay-side wall. The center half of the bin was covered with flooring, but the two ends were open, perfect for making kamikaze-like leaps through a maze of spider webs into the soft oats below.

Dad bought a hay baler. The haymow was soon filled with fifty-pound bales of alfalfa, strewn where they had fallen from the overhead carrier. The bales sometimes piled high against a board chute that surrounded the opening to the loft. We had to continue up the wall ladder inside the chute until we reached the top level of the bales.

We scaled the Everest of hay, looking for paths to the top or across the rough terrain to the distant oats bin. We hid in natural caverns or descended in deep chasms along the wall. We played hide and seek and tag and dragged the heavy bales to make forts and castles.

Mom let us camp in the haymow. We pushed a wad of sheets and blankets up the hole ahead of us and spread them out on a level area. We slept in our clothes. We talked and talked, a little afraid. The yellowish flyspecked light bulb was switched off, and we listened to the night sounds: the rustling of the pigeons, the creaking, cooling tin siding, and the shrinking roof boards. The horses stomped softly in the manger below.

We whispered. Then fell asleep.

Mom gave a little sigh as we dragged the dirty, barn-smelling bedding through the kitchen door.

Me, Arlo, and Marlys.
The little barn is on the left and the big barn on the right.

LUMBERYARD

The block-long Hage Lumberyard was located a short distance west of our school. Its contents were blocked from view on the west by an office building and along the street by a tall block wall. Only on the interior sides did a six-foot chain-link fence offer a tantalizing glimpse of the yard's potential.

One noon we were prowling the perimeter and discovered a kid-sized hole along the eastern end. Three of us squirmed single file under the fence and began cautiously exploring the grounds. We slinked from lumber pile to lumber pile, working our way toward the large storage building. We peeked through the open door. Spread before us was a lumber wonderland.

Two layers of storage bins flanked a wide central alley. At each side and at each end, steps led to walkways that fronted the upper levels. High above, a narrow catwalk arched between the two sides.

No one was in sight. Lumberyard workers apparently went home for dinner.

We raced up the steps and across the catwalk. We examined the bins. The potential for forts and hideouts seemed unlimited. The distant school bell rang. We hurried down the steps, under the fence, and back to our fourth-grade classroom. We were definitely on to something special. The secret would need to be guarded, shared only with our most trusted friends.

Our small group returned several days in a row. We played tag and built castles deep within the darkened bins. We armed ourselves with shields and spears and fought epic battles.

"Hey! What are you kids doing in here?"

No response. It is hard to talk while running at top speed.

White-eyed glances. He was after us. He could run pretty fast for an old guy.

The struggle was Darwinian; six kids cannot pass through a small hole at the same time. Due to starting position or foot speed, someone was destined to be last.

We dived and wiggled, Jerry Broulette at the rear. The man grabbed him by the back of the shirt. Jerry's adrenaline-driven response was immediate and remarkable; he twisted toward his captor and began to swear. Who knew a boy that age could possess such an extensive and colorful vocabulary?

To our credit we did not abandon our companion. We stood outside the fence, watching and listening in awe. Whether from compassion or shock, Jerry was released.

Harsh warnings pursued us as we raced for the school.

THE CART

I was nine the summer I found a pair of steel wheels in the weeds near the north edge of our farmstead. With the enthusiasm of a Hittite warrior, I began building a fearsome battle chariot. I must admit my construction skills failed to produce the product originally envisioned.

I located a wooden peach crate for the body, a short stick to use as an axle, and a longer pole to serve as the tongue on which to harness my imaginary steeds. I fastened the axle to the bottom of the body and drove a long nail through each end to keep the wheels from slipping off. The result was the perfect example of a "square peg in a round hole." The tongue was soon fastened in place and I was ready for battle.

I raced around the farm pulling my new vehicle between my legs. The fact that the wheels wobbled and squeaked or that the square tongue was slightly uncomfortable in my crotch in no way diminished my enthusiasm or curbed my adventures.

A day or two after completing my cart, I was climbing around on the far side of our silo and overheard my dad and our hired man, Herb, chuckling as they worked at repairing a piece of farm equipment. I don't remember their exact words, but the gist of the conversation was that my new vehicle was nothing but a pile of junk.

I pulled my cart behind the machine shed and smashed it to pieces.

Arlo is in the cart. Behind is Herb's car and the little house where our hired men and their families lived.

Bubblegum

I was in fourth grade. We finished our lunch and made our usual trip uptown. From more than a block away we could see a large crowd gathered in front of Ad's Variety Store. Here was something you didn't see every day.

My friends and I hurried over to see what the excitement was all about. Ad had obtained a shipment of bubblegum! I had no idea what bubblegum was. The war had been over for several years, but sugar and latex were still rationed and in short supply; much of our economy was still geared toward the aid and recovery of Europe and Asia.

Ad was selling the gum for two cents a stick with a restriction of one per customer; not a concern for me, as I didn't have two cents. Marlys was standing near the back of the crowd with Bonnie Engel and some of their friends, each clutching a newly purchased treasure. Bonnie's words went something like this, "Wayne, would you go in and buy a stick of bubblegum?" Of course, in the excitement of the moment I heard, "Wayne, my old friend, I'd like to buy you a stick of bubblegum."

I palmed her two pennies and joined the long line, finally making my transaction. I unwrapped the gum as I walked toward the door; I clearly remember my first smell of the sweet bubblegum fragrance. I walked down the steps and bit down on the hard wad. Bonnie gave a short gasp. Indignantly she snatched the gum from my mouth and the wax paper wrapper from my hand, made a few futile attempts to brush away my teeth marks with the back of her sleeve, and rewrapped the gum. The girls turned and walked toward school.

I had been used as a gum mule.

Horse

I can't remember if horse was a spring sport or a fall sport; in any case, it wasn't the namby-pamby game involving a basketball. Our horse was highly physical and involved a horse and a rider. The rider, usually a smaller participant, would ride on the shoulders of his larger team member, the horse. The object of the game was to topple the opposing teams. The rules were quite simple and can be easily summed up as "anything goes." Pushing, pulling, and charging were a few of the methods used to send the competition crashing to the ground.

Adding to the excitement was the fact that a typical match might involve up to a half-dozen horse and rider pairs, resulting in a veritable demolition derby of animal flesh. I'm sure you can imagine some of the strategies that were employed: blindsiding, ganging up, and the cowardly "lurking off to the side" approach.

Any team that crashed was eliminated from the contest. The game eventually ended with, what I suppose could be thought of as, "the last horse standing."

Dick Blue and I were a team. Dick was strong and a good athlete; I was small and wiry. Neither of us had enough common sense to respect or fear our opponents. This combination of traits made us formidable competitors in the horse pits.

My longest lasting memory of horse competition occurred on a day when Dick and I were matched against Gary Blickum and his rider. Gary was about the biggest kid in our grade and the battle was titanic. A final flurry of activity sent both teams crashing to the ground. I landed in an awkward position, and Gary and his rider landed on the back of my elbow. I was made acutely aware of the fact that elbows are intended to bend in one direction only. Sadly, the resulting injury not only ended my horse season but my entire softball season as well.

An Unfortunate Event

The summer I was ten I had a small flock of Muscovy ducks: five or six hens and two drakes. One of the drakes was a large black-and-white bird with an ugly, red-wattled face. He bullied his flock mates and lowered his head and hissed whenever I came near. I decided he must be eliminated.

A ten-year-old boy can run slightly faster than a flightless Muscovy duck. Armed with a sturdy club, I rushed into the flock and, with a dull thud, struck the victim a firm blow on the head. He failed to die but instead ran off with his terrified mates. I pursued and struck again with the same results, except that this time his head began to bleed.

I was caught in something far over my head but could see no way out.

Terror and panic overwhelmed me as I rushed about my grisly task. With tears flowing down my cheeks, I raced in to strike again and again. Finally he was down, and I rained blow after blow on his motionless body. Crying uncontrollably, I picked up his body and threw it into the weeds behind the barn.

Nightmares can persist. Sometimes they follow a young boy into adulthood.

THRESHING

There was a time when neighbors worked together in large communal groups to thresh their oats and wheat. I wasn't old enough to participate in these threshing runs, but I do remember accompanying my mother when she took morning lunch to the field. Our car was stuffed with mounds of sandwiches, pans of frosted brownies, jugs of hot coffee, and jars of Watkins Orange Nectar. We spread a large blanket on the oats stubble and displayed our wares for the hungry workers.

The teams were watered and their canvas nosebags filled with oats. The horses stomped their hooves and shook and rattled their leather fly nets as they methodically chewed the grain. The men filled their plates and cups and sat on the ground or dangled their legs over the side of a hayrack.

The harvesters rested for a short time after lunch, finishing their coffee and relaxing. They talked and twirled a long straw between their teeth or sprawled on their backs with a sweaty straw hat pulled over their face. Eventually one would drawl, "Well," and another would respond, "Yup," or, "I guess," and the men would slowly drag themselves upright.

Our big Case tractor was started, the clutch engaged, and the wide flat-belt began to flap and whine. The monstrous threshing machine was soon grinding and blowing away. The men with full racks began feeding it fat bundles of oats, while the rest of the teams returned to the field to refill their wagons. Mother covered the last remains with a dishtowel and loaded the car, and we bounced across the stubble toward the house.

The noon meal was an even greater event. The men removed their caps, revealing brown and white forehead lines. They all washed their hands, faces, and sunburned necks in the same large washbasin and dried their wet parts with an ever-dirtier towel. They combed back their hair, beat some of the dust from their pant legs, and walked into the house.

All the boards had been inserted into our large dining room table. Still, there was barely enough room to hold the mounds of food and the rows of bib-overalled men. Mother and one or two neighbor girls continually replaced the empty platters and tried to keep the bottomless coffee cups filled. The meal ended with an offering of two kinds of homemade pie. The men nodded, thanked my mom, and filed out the door.

A couple of years later, Dad bought a Case self-propelled combine with a loud Wisconsin engine and, for us, the threshing run was ended.

THE KETTLE IN UNDERWEAR

My brother Arlo is five years younger than me. He was five years old the summer he became the "Kettle in Underwear."

In the late forties and early fifties, Marjorie Main and Percy Kilbride starred as Ma and Pa Kettle in a series of slapstick, hillbilly movies. In the 1950 movie, *Ma and Pa Kettle Go to Town*, Pa has won a jingle contest that includes an all-expenses-paid trip to New York City. During their stay, Pa is mistaken for a wealthy industrialist who owns the Kettle Underwear Company. At one point, Pa is standing in his fancy hotel room in his ever-present long johns, when he receives a phone call from a man asking if he is the Kettle in underwear. Pa quizzically drawls, "How did you know?" and walks over to the window and closes the drapes.

We returned home from watching the movie and I began a program of slowly and insidiously teasing my brother. Whenever I saw him in his underwear I would call him the "Kettle in Underwear." I would repeat the phrase incessantly, making him more and more angry. My parents foolishly thought if they ignored the problem I would move on to some other form of torment.

I didn't.

My dad had finally had enough. He took me aside one day and told me he didn't ever again want to hear me call Arlo the "Kettle in Underwear." The next day when we were outside, I whispered to Arlo, "Whenever I pull on my ear, that means you're the Kettle in Underwear."

That night as Arlo was getting ready for bed, I slipped into his room and gave my ear a firm tug. Arlo exploded in rage, rushing across the room and biting me on the arm, leaving a perfect set of teeth marks. I let out a holler, and for the first and only time I remember, Dad lost his temper and spanked one of us. Arlo.

I knew who deserved the spanking and who really was the "Kettle in Underwear."

Snow Day

I don't know why I hated going to school; I never found it overly disagreeable once I got there. There were really only two ways to avoid the inevitable. One was to feign illness, an art I eventually became so good at that I could occasionally fool my mother into letting me stay home. The second required less work on my part and far more on the part of Mother Nature: I needed a blizzard.

Storms came without warning in the days before the National Weather Bureau, satellites, and sophisticated media meteorologists. The first hints often came in the form of a damp northeast wind. Heavy snows would begin to fall and, as the storm moved eastward, were followed by northwest gales and dropping temperatures.

My last act before going to bed was to open the porch door, stare at the yard light, and feel and listen to the storm's fury. Good storms would dim and, from time to time, completely block out the light.

My bedroom was on the west side of our house. We had no windbreak on our farm, and the unobstructed wind howled and moaned as it rattled the windows and drove the snow against the siding. Strong gusts threatened to shake the entire structure from its foundation.

I pulled the quilts around my head and listened to and felt the raging storm, carefully planning how I, if lost in the woods or a traveling pioneer boy, would build a shelter, start a cozy fire, and comfortably survive the blizzard.

Eventually I would drift into a dreamless sleep, secure in the knowledge there would be no school tomorrow.

I still feel the same thrill and excitement from an imminent or raging storm, even though I know that when it's over I will face hours of cold and discomfort sitting on my tractor, scooping out my driveway and farmyard.

Tiling

Farm fields, or at least the lower, wetter parts, are usually underlain with drainage tile. Excess water is carried from the land through an ever-larger system of tile until it eventually flows into an open drainage ditch or river system.

Nowadays, fields are tiled with large, self-propelled machines and long tubes of porous plastic drainage tile, but when I was a small boy trenches were dug and cement tiles laid by hand. I was fortunate to witness the last hand tiling done on my father's farm and perhaps some of the last anywhere. I was ten years old when Dad hired John Helgo's crew to tile a few acres of wetland in the northeast corner of our farm.

John ran the level and supervised the job, while his crew of three dug the trench and laid the tiles. I sometimes hear the term ditch digger used in a derogatory way; on that day I acquired an appreciation for the skill and art involved in that profession.

The men's narrow tiling spades were unbelievably polished and shiny from thousands of cuts into the soil. At any pause in their work, an oily cloth appeared and was rubbed over the metal surface to prevent even a hint of rust from forming. It was critical that the shovel "scour" and the dirt slide off effortlessly with each toss. The men worked backwards in single file, moving in the direction indicated by the surveyor. The first man cut a trench a foot deep, the length of his spade, and three spade widths wide. The second and third men followed the first, each deepening the ditch another foot. At regular intervals they paused, produced a sharpening stone from their mud-covered overalls, and gave the cutting edge of their spade a few quick passes. Their collective work was amazing; they seemed to move across the field as a single, well-oiled machine.

John crept along with an old flatbed truck, and the men unloaded foot-long cement tiles next to one edge of the ditch. The men began laying the tile as soon as the truck was unloaded. The six-inch diameter tiles were handed down and positioned end to end at the bottom of the ditch, each gently tamped into place. Narrow gaps, the correct width to allow water to drain into the tile line but still keep dirt out, were left between each tile. One following crewmember shaved the edge of the trench with his spade and covered the tile with several inches of loose dirt to hold them in place. I jumped back and forth across the open trench or peered over the edge and watched the men work, generally making a nuisance of myself.

All the branches were eventually completed and spliced into a larger main line that carried the water farther down the system. The next day, Dad drove our small Case tractor to the field and pushed the ridges of loose dirt back into the trenches. He told me that, over time, small seams would open in the soil, allowing floodwater to drain quickly to the tiles and greatly improve their efficiency.

When I left the farm more than ten years later, rows of clay-colored subsoil still marked the lines where John and his crew had toiled with their spades.

Herb

Herb was a big man: six foot six. In summer, the two most important jobs for a hired man on our farm were baling hay and cultivating corn. Herb was good at both. He could stand on the ground and, seemingly without effort, throw bales several rows high on the hayrack. There were no weed-killing chemicals or genetically engineered seed corn. Weeds could be controlled in only one way: with cultivation. Most years, the fields were covered five times. This meant that within a few days of completing all the fields, it would be time to repeat the process. Herb would take our DC Case tractor with its four row cultivator and begin early in the morning. Except for a short noon break, he would work until supper, always attempting to cultivate eighty acres a day.

Many evenings he would come out of the little house where he and his wife Laverne lived, I'm sure hoping to walk around and relax after his hard day's work. Instead, there I was. "Herb, will you walk around the slough with me?" I know now how tired he must have been, but he almost always consented.

Down through the pasture. We always turned to the right at the slough and made the circuit counter-clockwise. Herb was quiet and gentle and tried to answer my never-ending questions. He may not have been a trained naturalist or philosopher, but he seemed wise to me. Some sections of the walk, overgrazed pastureland, were easy to navigate, but part of the way we had to slog through tall marsh weeds and grasses, making the going more difficult. There were always interesting things to see: a swimming muskrat with a cattail tuber in its mouth, a pair of mallards bobbing near shore, or a tall, skinny slough-pump, its beak straight up, trying to blend in with the vertical marsh grass and cattail stalks.

A half hour or forty-five minutes later, our expedition completed, we would trudge back up the hill to the farm. I doubt if I ever thanked Herb.

I was quite small the summer I found a firecracker on the street. I was preparing to light it one evening in front of the barn when Herb happened by. After a short lecture on the dangers I was confronting, he proceeded to demonstrate the correct procedure. He pulled a big, wooden farmer's match from his pocket, struck it on the button of his bib overalls, lit the fuse, and quickly threw the firecracker. Nothing. Herb carefully explained to me that this was a most critical time; the fire could smolder for a long while. Finally, after an acceptable waiting period and it was safe to do so, he picked up the firecracker. It exploded! I remember Herb walking around for several weeks with an ugly black thumbnail. Lesson learned.

Herb was very frugal and, after working for Dad several years, saved up enough money to buy a marginally productive farm a few miles north of Henderson, Minnesota. Much of his high ground was on the bluffs overlooking the Minnesota River, too hilly for anything more than low-grade pasture. His remaining land was on the floodplain where his crops often drowned. In spite of these difficulties, Herb and Laverne were able to raise a fine family and live out their lives on their farm. Things were never quite the same on ours.

Gang War

A neighborhood battle was imminent. The James brothers had recruited me as a mercenary. Lance, Louis, and Phillip lived across the street from the gymnasium, and their adversaries were headquartered two blocks to the west, on the far side of the school playground. Trouble had been brewing all summer.

Secret plans were hatched and battlefield tactics developed. Our side spent hours becoming fluent in Pig Latin, a tactic sure to provide a critical advantage during the heat of battle. In the unlikely event the fortunes of war turned against us, we had established a backup plan. We would retreat to an impregnable tree house fortress in the James' backyard.

Lacking molten tar to pour down on our pursuers, we settled for the next best option. Ducks had laid several clutches of eggs in an old building behind the machine shed on our farm. Some of the nests had been abandoned and, in others, only a few of the eggs had hatched. All those that remained were rotten. I carefully wrapped and transported these critical chemical weapons in my bike basket, and we transferred them to the tree house.

One day, as we were continuing our plans, the unthinkable happened. The opposing army showed up in force. Toe to toe and puffed chest to puffed chest, we hurled insults and issued threats. The tension gradually diffused and each side turned away, convinced they had finally shown "those other guys."

School neared, and we entered the throes of a late August heat wave. I had a dentist appointment and was greeted by Dr. James. "Aneway!" It was his normal salute, in reference to my linguistic prowess, but lacked its usual friendliness.

Heat had caused the duck eggs to explode, their putrefying liquids seeping through the tree house floor and down the trunk of the apple tree.

A menacing drill, grinding deep in my mouth, prevented me from responding.

Taboo

Laura Ingalls, Tom Sawyer, or the Hardy Boys never once used an outhouse or found it necessary to slip behind a tree. Writers of stories about young people were careful to avoid the topic of human excretion.

My Uncle Ed owned a farm a few miles north of us. Part of his land was located on the bottom of an old lakebed. The peat soil was usually too wet to plow and was overgrown with dense stands of wild-growing reed canary grass. My father decided to mow and bale this grass for cattle feed, a process that required several days working in humid, near one-hundred-degree temperatures. I tagged along.

While Dad and Herb mowed, raked, baled, and stacked a mountain of coarse hay, I explored the abandoned farm buildings, climbed and wandered a high wooded island that projected above the former lakebed, or laid around in the shady woods.

Nature called. I collected a handful of dry, soft leaves and found an out-of-the-way place among the trees.

What I saw next was foreign and fascinating and flew in the face of my elementary school science education. Insects were supposed to metamorphose through the stages of egg, larvae, pupa, and adult. Before I could cover the evidence of my recent activity, my feces were swarming with flies. These were no ordinary flies. White, fully operational maggots were being ejected from the end of their abdomens. I watched in fascination as the little creatures wiggled and burrowed through their freshly discovered medium.

I now know these acquaintances belonged to a family of ovoviviparous organisms called flesh flies. Insects of this type hatch their eggs and store their offspring internally, so they are instantly available to take advantage of newly discovered carrion or other organic material.

I'm surprised my newfound fascination didn't lead me to a profession in entomology. Or one in scatology.

Frank And Florence

It was the mid-thirties, and the Great Depression had been grinding on for several years. Dad placed an advertisement in the Minneapolis newspaper for a new hired man. The next morning, cars were lined up for several blocks down our gravel road. Like a scene from *Grapes of Wrath*, many of the vehicles were piled high with household goods and their interiors packed with family members and personal possessions.

Dad struggled through the interview process, overwhelmed by the numbers and the desperation of the applicants. He completed the interviews, selected his new help, and dismissed those still in line. Job seekers continued to arrive for several more days. Dad swore he would never again place an ad in a newspaper, and he never did.

After enduring the discomfort of the hiring process, Dad ended up selecting the worst worker of the entire group. The new man was fired during his first week on the job.

Thank goodness for second choices. Frank and Florence Hoffman, a young married couple from Hancock, Minnesota, soon arrived at Dad's farm. They moved into the "Little House," the only building remaining from our farm's previous owners, the Peels. Frank turned out to be an excellent worker and, more importantly, Florence had a younger sister, Hilda, who often came to visit.

The romance between my father and Hilda, while true, had its rocky moments. At one point Dad broke off the relationship, convinced the difference in their ages was too great an obstacle to overcome.

Frank and Florence returned to Hancock in the late thirties and purchased a farm of their own. Mom and Dad married and had us kids. The bond between the two families remained strong, and the long road between Madelia and Hancock was traveled several times each year.

The never-ending question of my youth seemed to be, "Are we there yet?" Google Maps tells me it is one hundred forty-five miles and takes two hours, forty-three minutes to drive from Madelia to Hancock. I suppose the miles are correct, but the time is far from accurate. The trip was neverending.

The first half was bearable; the route as far as Olivia was often varied, and fatigue had yet to set in. When we reached Willmar, US Highway 12 angled to the northwest, a straight ribbon with an unending jumble of small towns.

Finally the abandoned brick schoolhouse at Clontarf, with its enclosed, playground-like spiral fire escape, came into view. It was time to begin looking for Frank's barn.

A half mile before Hancock, Highway 12 made a sharp left and disappeared under the Great Northern railroad embankment. To the right of the underpass, on the north side of the gravel road, Frank's red barn peeked from behind his windbreak.

In summer we were mobbed at the car and in winter welcomed as we stomped into the kitchen, flooded in the warmth of an iron and porcelain cook stove.

Winter nights, the adults played pinochle or schmear, pounding down their winning tricks and arguing as they rehashed each hand. We played games until we were exhausted or until told it was bedtime. Florence would spread quilts on the dining room floor in front of the brown enamel oil-burning stove. We were covered with blankets and told to calm down and go to sleep.

We squirmed and whispered. The burning fuel oil gave off a soft murmur, and yellow light flickered and danced through a small isinglass window. We awoke to the sound and smell of frying bacon.

Florence had cut thick slices from a slab of home-cured bacon. The strips bubbled and spattered in a big cast iron pan, finally emerging curled and crisp. The bacon was set aside and kept warm on the back of the stove, while large brown eggs were cracked and emptied into the pool of grease. Each addition triggered a new round of crackling and sputtering.

The eggs weren't turned. Hot grease was spread over the yolks with a spatula; the tops turned shiny white and the edges a crispy brown. Finally they were given a liberal shake from Florence's large-holed salt and pepper shakers.

Stacks of oven toasted homemade bread and a dish of freshly churned butter waited on her thick-legged kitchen table. We were fed in the order we awoke. I ate with two hands, dipping a piece of toast into a black-flecked egg with one and clutching a thick slice of bacon in the other.

A two-holed outhouse was located a short distance from the house. Use was postponed as long as possible. Below zero in winter, and fly infested and smelly in summer, reading or dawdling was not an option. I tried to imagine a scenario in which both holes would be used at the same time.

Frank milked. His pastures were north of the farm, reached by the cows through long, barbed wired lanes. Sometimes the cows came to the barn at milking time, but often they had to be herded home. Marlys and I were allowed to help. Some days the multicolored cows streamed ahead of us, anxious for the extra feed they received at milking time; other days they stubbornly resisted, munching at each clump of grass or sticking their heads through the wire fence, straining to steal corn from Frank's fields.

One dry summer, when the pastures were nearly depleted, we went out in midafternoon and slowly herded the cattle home along a small township road between Frank's fields and the Great Northern tracks. They were allowed to take their time and eat their fill of the free grass. The cows calmly ignored the loud steam engines and long trains that shook the embankment and filled the air with deafening noise.

The cows were milked by hand and the fresh milk carried in pails to the milk room where it was poured into a separator. A long crank was turned by hand and the milk forced through a tall stack of internal stainless steel cones. Blue-looking skim milk ran from one spout and a much smaller stream of yellow cream from another. Turning the separator crank looked like fun. It turned out to be boring and far more strenuous than it looked. After a few minutes I was happy to turn the job back to the experts.

The cream was placed in special cream cans and stored in a tank of cool water at the base of the windmill. The skim was poured into long wooden troughs and fought over by rows of squealing pigs.

Twice a week, Frank hauled the cream to the creamery in Hancock. The monthly check he received was the farm's primary source of income.

One summer I was puzzled to find burlap bags filled with milkweed pods hanging in their garage. Sherwood and his older sister Geraine had been collecting them for the war effort. Japanese expansion in the Pacific had cut off America's source of kapok, a fiber used to make life preservers. The milkweed fluff was being collected by school children across the country to be used as a substitute.

We rode low-hanging willow branch horses, climbed in the haymow, explored distant woodlots, and ate wild onion tubers. Sherwood, three years older, drew from a wide repertoire of jokes, many off-color, and seemed able to invent exciting new activities at will.

Too soon our two or three day visit would come to an end. We stood around the car talking, prolonging the inevitable departure. One member of our family often cried in disappointment as we drove down Frank and Florence's driveway but, soon exhausted, fell sound asleep.

The Book Report

We were fairly warned. The first book reports of the year would begin Monday. Miss Lenz employed a diabolical selection procedure: she would call on us randomly. The hour-long English period could accommodate about six reports.

Monday arrived and the ordeal began. We all held our breath and stared at our desktops, attempting to shrink into the least conspicuous form. Sweaty palms stained our wide-lined report outlines.

One by one the lambs were called to the slaughter. No one listened to the reports; they were too busy calculating the number that remained and the odds of being the next one called. The time we were spending could have more appropriately been applied to arithmetic.

"Wayne, you're next."

Red-faced and clammy, I made my way to the front.

"My book is *Tarzan of the Apes* by Edgar Rice Burroughs."

I held an advantage over many of my peers: I loved to read. Thanks to my mother, I had haunted the local library for as long as I could remember, devouring and discarding one new genre after another.

Tarzan was one of the good books, its story a convoluted tale of adventure and survival. The action moved and twisted from ape to man and continually changed in time and location, from Gorgo the water buffalo to Tantor the elephant, from grassland to savanna to rainforest.

I haltingly worked my way through my half-memorized outline. Slowly a change came over me as I became caught up in the excitement of the story. Each detail and conversation became crystal clear. I became the giant apes swinging through the trees; I fought battles to protect the orphaned boy and helped him learn the meaning of the strange symbols in the books in the long-forgotten cabin. I told it all!

Miss Lenz let me go on and on, well into the next subject period. The class was carried along with the tale and I could feel the excitement growing in them as well.

We gave three more book reports that year, and I remember enjoying each of my presentations.

Summers were long in the early fifties, allowing plenty of time to forget. Miss McCarthy called me to the front for my first sixth-grade book report. I was as terrified as if fifth grade had never happened. I never again became fully comfortable in front of a class or group of people until I grew up and became a teacher.

Snowball Fight

There were different kinds of snowball fights. Some were malicious affairs where certain groups or grades deserved and received their proper punishment; others were territorial. To wit: the titanic cross-street battles between St. Mary's and our public school. Our most common form of contest, however, was the ritualized "battle for the cannon."

An old World War I cannon stood chained to a cement platform near the north end of the playground. One team would be selected to defend the gun while an opposing team attacked and tried to drive them away in humiliating retreat. After a major battle, the teams would often switch position, the attackers now the defenders.

One problem was that our battles were deemed unfair; Dick Blue and I always managed to get on the same team. Since we refused to retreat, our cannon-guarding corps would usually rally around us and the weapon was securely held. When we were the attackers, we would simply rush up to the cannon and employ the snowballer's version of hand-to-hand combat. We would throw a flurry of projectiles point blank at our opponent's faces until they broke and ran.

Informed of our nefarious ways, and obviously supported by a certain group of poor losers, Miss Lenz devised a solution. A day of perfect snowball weather arrived. She announced, before dismissing us for recess, that we would choose sides for our ensuing battle and that Dick and I would be captains, thus ensuring we would be on opposing teams.

Looking back, I can only assume that one or more of the following must have been the truth: Dick was a better snowballer than me, he was a better judge of snowball talent, or he was a finer leader of men. In any case, the battle proved to be a disaster for me, my team, and I suppose, ultimately, my reputation.

My team was selected to defend. Without hesitation, Dick, employing our usual method of attack, rushed his hordes forward into battle. After a few pathetic counter throws, my army broke and ran. I was quickly surrounded and pelted unmercifully at close range while I frantically tried to return fire. Suddenly, as if by some mysterious signal, the firing ceased and the grim looks on the faces around me faded to ones of pity, or perhaps of bland resignation. The battle was ended and, strangely, along with it, the fifth graders' enthusiasm for snowball fighting.

Tackle Tag

Pump-pump-pull-away is a time-honored children's game. The playing field is bounded by a rectangle; the two longer sides form the goals and the shorter ends are the out-of-bound lines. Our field was marked at each corner by a large tree and enclosed an area similar to a double length basketball court.

The rules are simple. One player is "it," and all the other players line up on one of the goal lines. At a given signal, all must run across the field to the opposite goal, attempting to avoid being touched by "it." If touched, they join the increasing numbers in that group until eventually all have been touched, at which time the game has ended and a new one begins. The signal to send the players running supposedly was, "Pump-pump-pull-away, come away or I'll pull you away." In our case this was simply reduced to, "Go."

I believe this is an appropriate time to discuss the variability in human development, one that impacts this and many of my playground stories. Typically, as boys develop into young men, they show marked increases in size, strength, and running speed. My development, which occurred later than most of my peers, involved only two of the above. For some strange reason, I became slower as I grew older, at least in relation to my peers. My years of being faster and more agile than most of my classmates were short lived. It was as if I had unwittingly, in the words of songwriter Kris Kristofferson, "traded in tomorrow for today."

Tackle tag is pump-pump-pull-away's mean older brother on steroids. As the name implies, no sissy touching is involved; players are tackled, pushed, or tripped, all legal methods of depositing a competitor flat on the ground. Players so positioned now become part of the tackling team.

Early in the game, when there is one, or just a few, on the tackling team, crossing is a breeze. One can cockily skip, prance, or jog across, knowing that the "it" group will concentrate on slower, easier marks. Gradually, crossing becomes more precarious as the numbers in the center grow. Now guile and strategy come into play; one can make a quick dash for it before the mob is organized or cross in an area covered by slower or less aggressive tacklers.

On days when things were going well, one could attain the somewhat dubious honor of being the last man standing. Luckily, the great rush of adrenaline needed to face a mob of twenty determined tacklers usually accompanies this honor. What to do but go! Dodging, cutting, and weaving, you race for the far goal, sometimes miraculously surviving a pass or two, but ultimately being crushed by a mass of humanity.

WILSON'S WOODS

A mile west of our farm, Elm Creek flowed south to the Watonwan River. The far side was pastureland where Martin Snyder's purebred Angus herd grazed the hillsides and, on hot days, wandered down to drink and stand belly deep in the muddy stream in a futile attempt to avoid the annoying insects of summer.

Our side of the creek was different. A two-hundred-yard band of second-growth forest stretched for a mile north to the shores of Wilson's Lake. None of us kids knew who the Wilsons were. Only the senior members of our family remembered they had sold out and moved away in the twenties, their name all that remained. Bob Mosser and his family lived along the shore of the lake and owned the woods. Occasionally, Bob would allow a few cattle to graze, but for the most part we considered the woods unclaimed territory.

One early summer day, when I was nine, my older sister Marlys and her friend Cheryl laid out a plan to explore the woods. I quickly attached myself to the expedition. With our eyes on the distant tree line and a picnic basket in hand, we trudged along our old dirt field road, then the township gravel, finally reaching our destination. I remember only a few specifics about our exploration that day: the field tile that discharged its small stream into the creek, our careful observations to make sure we didn't get lost, and a large tree staggering under a burden of grapevines. Here we ate our lunch, a place Marlys and Cheryl christened "The Arbor."

It wasn't the specifics that were important. I had discovered a wondrous new world, a place of unlimited adventure. I roamed, camped, and built shelters and hideouts. I constructed a tower of logs and branches that nearly touched the sky. I smoked cigarettes, played with fire, and ran semi-naked along the cow paths, wearing only an Indian breechclout. Here I hunted and trapped and saw my first white-tailed deer, an animal then almost unheard of in southern Minnesota. As I write this, I am looking at a badge of honor: an inch-long scar across the top of my left hand I received while driving a stake into the ground with a coke bottle. I still think it strange that I could see the tendons and tissues deep in my hand and not shed a single drop of blood.

One adventure stands above all others. A barbed wire fence crossed the creek near the south end of the woods. Here Snyder's cattle had stomped out and widened a small muddy pond. Someone had dragged in and abandoned an old leaky rowboat, a craft promptly commandeered by my friends and me. The owners, not having the courtesy to provide us with oars, forced us to hunt up push poles from the woods. Making progress required equal amounts of poling and bailing, the latter accomplished with a rusty coffee can. After two or three short shakedown cruises, the day arrived for our big adventure; we would take her to the headwaters. What could be more enjoyable than a quiet voyage around Wilson's Lake?

My shipmate for the voyage was my friend Jim Sorenson. It was a hot, muggy, midsummer day. We came armed with sturdy push poles, a new bailing can, and the requisite amount of enthusiasm. The problem with propelling a heavy boat up a muddy stream with poles is that they sink into the mud with each push. The effort of pulling the pole out of the mud retards forward motion and pulls the boat backwards. Facing a slow current, in combination with the mud, made progress far more difficult than we had anticipated.

It was over a half mile to the lake. The encroachment of cattails and rushes began to narrow the creek. The main stream gradually disappeared and we were forced to choose among several lesser channels. Even these closed as we neared the lake, and we began pushing the craft over and through the vegetation.

We were close; soon we would break through to open water. We stood on the edges of the boat, trying to see it. The composition of the vegetation changed; suddenly we faced a dense wall of wiry bulrush. The afternoon sun beat into the still marsh. Mosquitoes swarmed over our sweating bodies, and the smell of rotten marsh gas filled our nostrils. The boat was no longer afloat; it rode on a sea of compressed rushes.

We could hear the lapping of waves on the lake. The push poles sank deep into the mud as we applied our full weight; the boat remained stationary. We were defeated.

If one cannot go forward and cannot stay, one must go back. Sensible, but far easier said than done. Square-sterned crafts resist going backward. Eventually, with much tugging and pulling on the reeds, pushing with our poles, and throwing our weight forward and back, we were able to break free, turn around, and begin our voyage home. We floated and poled with the current, retraced our recently traveled path, and returned to our point of embarkation. Hot, tired, and thirsty, we abandoned our craft, and with it, our love of sailing.

THE JOKE

It is said the key to telling a good joke is timing, timing, timing. Another key I was about to learn is, "know your audience."

My Uncle Ed stopped by our house one evening when I was in fourth grade and asked if I wanted to go roller skating. He already had a couple of kids in his car, so I piled in beside them. We stopped in Searles and picked up Marilyn and Ardis Splinter; the Splinters were good friends of Ed's.

We were heading for the New Ulm Armory. This large building had a slate floor that was excellent for skating; on weekend nights, when not being used to train warriors, it was opened for community use. My skating experience was limited to circling our basement furnace, skates clamped to my oxfords with the help of a big metal skate key. Certainly I was ready for the big time.

Uncle Ed bought our tickets, paid for our skate rental, and left us on our own. It didn't take long to master the straightaways; the curves were a little tougher, requiring a delicate balance between gravitational pull and centrifugal force. Leaning into the curve caused the skates to slide outward, dumping you on your hip. Standing too upright threw your whole body against the wall. All of this had to be learned, of course, while skating as fast as humanly possible.

Music blared from speakers mounted at each end of the rink. Between songs, an announcer suddenly broke in: "The next skate will be ladies' choice." I had even less experience with girls than I did with roller skating. Marilyn grabbed me by the hand and asked if I would skate with her. I was too flustered to say no. It turned out things were not so different from skating alone, except now I had a girl fastened to my sweaty palm. Once I figured out the trick of skating in the same rhythm as Marilyn, it was kind of fun; so fun in fact that we skated together much of the evening.

Ed rounded us up and we headed for home. We stopped at the Splinter's, and Marcella and Elmer invited us in for a cup of hot chocolate. There were a few whispers among the grownups, and suddenly the teasing began. Evidently skating with a girl was some sort of a hilarious taboo. I turned beet red.

Eventually it came down to this.

Elmer: "I suppose you are going to marry her?"

I could see things were rapidly deteriorating. I was being backed into a corner. I fancied myself quite the humorist; perhaps the best thing to do was fight fire with fire and go along with the joke.

Me: "I guess."

Adults don't think nine-year-old boys capable of sophisticated humor. The room roared. I was horrified; everyone thought I was serious.

You have to know your audience.

I met Marilyn in Madelia when we were in our late teens, and she gently reminded me of that long ago evening, still believing I had been serious.

Egos can be fragile at any age. The teasing of that evening, and the teasing by family members in similar events that followed, made it difficult for me to feel comfortable around girls for a very long time.

Swimming Lessons

My mother loved to swim; her fondest childhood memories were of spending summers at the lake with her nieces and cousins.

I hated swimming, not that I could actually do it. I was skinny and wiry with the specific gravity of a cannonball. Mother thought the easiest thing for me to learn would be the back float, a stroke she was a master of. She held me up and asked, "Are you ready?" She removed her hand from the small of my back and I promptly sank. "You have to arch your back." I arched as far as I could. I sank again. It was obvious I needed professional help.

School ended in late May, and swimming lessons began the following week. Monday dawned cold and cloudy. We climbed onto the crowded school bus and headed for Long Lake, close to the neighboring town of St. James, a twenty-mile trek. There was no competition for the beach. The St. James kids knew enough to wait until later in the summer when the ice had melted.

We were herded into the changing house and then down to the beach, where we were separated into groups with strange names. They got me into the water where I stood with my arms clutched to my chest. My transparent skin and lips turned blue as the whitecaps crashed over me. I began to shake uncontrollably, my body covered with goose bumps. I made a run for it.

I wrapped myself in my towel and huddled behind the changing house, hoping no one would find me. An eternity later they were still fooling around down at the lake. I wandered into the bathhouse and watched two boys trying to peek through a hole in the wall between the boys' and girls' changing rooms. A girl would shove a sharp pencil through the opening as soon as an eye approached.

Gradually, kids began wandering in and changing into their street clothes. We climbed on the bus, and I wrapped my shivering body in my towel and endured the endless trip home.

Mom was waiting for us at the bus stop. I climbed into the backseat. She turned and cheerfully asked, "How did your first day go?"

First Hunt

Anyone questioning the validity of natural selection hasn't had the opportunity to observe the evolution of the ring-necked pheasant. Once upon a time, pheasants escaped their predators like any self-respecting bird: they flew. The flyers are now mostly dead, taking with them the genes needed to pass on that outmoded method of escape. I was fortunate to grow up during the heyday of the flying ring-neck.

My sister Marlys was eleven and I was eight the first time I went pheasant hunting. The term "hunting" is loosely used here. My Uncle John and a group of his friends arrived at our farm one fall morning; they were planning to hunt the cornfield east of our house. Mar and I were invited to come along as fillers: we would walk in line with the gun-carrying grownups, helping to drive the birds toward the end of the field. We walked north, the dry corn leaves cutting and scratching our faces as we struggled to keep our place in line. From time to time a pheasant would flush, and the hunter nearest the fleeing bird would take a shot or two. As we approached the end of the quarter-mile field, all guns were raised in anticipation. Suddenly, at least from the perspective of a small boy, all hell broke loose. Clouds of pheasants burst into the air, guns blasted, feathers flew, and birds fell; those not hit flapped and glided across our alfalfa field to John's cornfield.

The hunters that crossed the fence to pick up the felled birds left their guns with comrades on our side. We made two more passes of the field, one down and one back. John and his friends returned to our farm, climbed back into their cars, and headed home, each having filled their five bird limits. Two large multicolored roosters were left on our doorstep.

I began my real pheasant hunting career as a criminal. Dad said I could hunt that fall. His only gun, an old single shot, sawed-off twenty gauge, had been left in the empty house on our other farm, probably used to shoot some kind of varmint. The day before the season opened, I walked the long mile across our dirt field road and picked up the gun and a pocketful of shells. I had never fired a shotgun. On the way home I practiced dry firing the gun. Cocking the hammer turned out to be a difficult chore for a small sixth grader.

A quarter mile from home I slipped a shell in the chamber, just to see how it felt to carry a loaded weapon. Suddenly, a big speckled hen burst from the edge of the road and angled across the corn. The law be damned. I hauled back the stubborn hammer, took careful aim, and fired, saved from a sure prison sentence by a spectacularly errant shot.

Intent to kill would be difficult to prove in a court of law.

Unlikely Hero

I was the ninth or tenth best ballplayer in my class, a ranking regularly affirmed by my peers through the time-honored "choose up sides" method. I was in fifth grade the year our class was challenged to a softball game by the sixth grade. Arrangements were made for this match to be played on the northwest diamond of our playground. The game was to last as many days as it took to complete nine innings. Interclass competitions were rare; the novelty of the event and, what turned out to be the closeness of the contest, stirred considerable fan interest. The score seesawed back and forth for three days. I didn't play the first two days, as Richard Ellingsberg caught those games. Rich and I were pretty equal in ability, and I ended up playing his position on the third day. I know this will seem unlikely, but in the bottom of the ninth, with our team trailing and with runners on base, I came to bat.

I can picture the pitch and my bat making contact with the ball. I didn't pull the ball to the shortstop side as I usually did but drove a hard grounder toward right field.

Ballplayers refer to a slow ground ball that finds an unlikely hole in the infield and trickles into the outfield as a "seeing-eye single." I hit a seeing-eye home run. The ball slipped between the first and second basemen and somehow eluded two outfielders long enough for me to round third and race home ahead of the throw.

I don't remember much about the congratulations I must have received on the field, but I do remember the thrill I got when we returned to Miss Lenz's classroom. Rich Uttech raised his hand and asked if he could tell what had happened at the game. He explained how he had been standing on the sidelines talking to a sixth grader when I came to bat. The sixth grader asked if I was any good, and Dick replied that I could sometimes "hit 'em pretty hard." I can still feel my face turn red and my chest swell with pride as the whole class turned to look at me.

I am a baseball fan and have watched piles of grown men jump on one of their teammates to celebrate his driving in or scoring a game-winning run. None of these men have ever felt happier than a certain skinny fifth grader in the spring of 1950.

Duck Hunting

Our farm was duck hunters' paradise; we had two marshes within a couple hundred yards of our house. In the days leading up to the season opener, I would head down to these sloughs after school and study my quarry. The breeding season had been a good one and mallard and teal were plentiful; they bobbed like corks as they fed in the marshy ponds. If I crept too close and became threatening, they simply flushed and flew the hundred yards across Lindstrom's pasture to the other slough. I noticed a pattern: they followed a shallow drainage ditch as they moved between the two marshes. The seeds of a plan began to grow. On opening day, I would hide at one end of the ditch. When the shooting began, the ducks would fly directly over me as they fled from slough to slough.

In the early fifties, the hunting season began at noon on Friday. I submitted the proper paperwork to my sixth-grade teacher, a note written by my mother, and watched the minute hand creep around the clock face, waiting for the eleven o'clock release time. I rushed out the west door where my Cousin Russell waited in his car. There was no time to waste. We drove to the farm where we picked up my sawed-off twenty gauge and a ragged cardboard box with ten shells, then walked through our pasture to the east slough. Russell chose for his blind a small clump of cattails straight down from our buildings. I casually commented I would move a little further to the right. I could see several other hunters, but luckily none had claimed my spot.

Ducks were becoming nervous and began flying back and forth between the sloughs. Not having a watch, I could only crouch and wait for someone else to begin shooting. Suddenly, it was twelve o'clock; gunfire seemed to explode from everywhere.

No one ever had a better plan. Ducks rushed back and forth along the ditch, directly over my blind. They came in singles, groups of three or four, or in small flocks. I drew a bead on a big drake and fired. He kept flying. A pair of teal zoomed down the ditch toward me. This time I really concentrated; again not a feather was disturbed. More ducks, more shots, the same results. By five minutes after twelve I was out of shells and had not harmed a single duck. The panicked ducks continued to zoom up and down my ditch. I ran back to Russell and asked if I could borrow some shells, not remembering his twelve gauge shells wouldn't fit my gun. I raced to the house and pleaded with my mom to take me to town to help me get more ammunition. She was too busy. How could anything be more important than this? I would gladly have ridden my bike to the Coast to Coast store, but Mom informed me they didn't sell ammunition to minors. I was beaten.

I wandered dejectedly back down to watch Russell hunt. He bagged a few ducks, but his spot was not well chosen; the ducks preferred the safety of my ditch. Soon the flying frenzy ended. The ducks departed our two small sloughs and headed for bigger and safer waters.

Hunting continued to be a great passion of mine for the next ten years. I became a respectable shot and brought home many more ducks than my mother cared to cook. In all the years I hunted, I never again found myself in the perfect place at the perfect time. I could have missed twenty or thirty more birds if I hadn't run out of shells.

WORKUP

This is an educational story. No self-respecting child should grow up without playing, or at least knowing how to play, workup.

I loved to play softball but my opportunities were restricted both geographically and culturally. I was a farm kid. Town kids called each other up or talked to each other and organized neighborhood ball games during the summer. Farm kids stayed home.

The sum of my playing experience involved occasionally getting together on weekends with the Ellingsberg kids or playing ball at school. School softball, "no baseballs allowed," was divided into three categories: morning ball, noon ball, and recess ball. Workup was morning ball.

I know from my adult experience that nice warm mornings in April and May are uncommon. The fact that they occurred frequently in my memory should in no way distract from this story.

I descend the stairs at seven o'clock sharp. Our daily breakfast guest, Dallas Townsend, is broadcasting the *World News Roundup* through the slots in our plastic kitchen counter radio. I eat a big bowl of Grape-Nuts, drink a glass of orange juice, throw on a light jacket, slide my glove over my handlebars, and head for town. You will notice there is no mention of schoolbooks.

My Schwinn bike is beginning to show, if not its age, at least the wear from years of unending abuse. I make no thought of its condition as I ride the gravel road leading to town, but once on the city streets I become acutely aware of its flaws. The raw sound of the front tire rubbing on the rattling fender and the loud click, faithfully broadcast with each revolution of the right pedal, is magnified on the quiet morning streets. Except for an occasional mailman, few are up to stare and cringe at this auditory affront. My biggest fear is that one of my classmates will witness my passing. I slink low beneath my cap as I coast past their houses. Fortunately, most town kids are late sleepers.

The janitors are earlier risers, and the school and classroom doors are unlocked. I slip into our dark cloakroom, dig through the old wooden box in the back corner, and come up with the least mushy ball and one or two uncracked bats.

I have my choice of any of several ball diamonds, but it makes little difference; I am the only one present. The only thing I can do is sit on one of the swings and wait. I never could understand, and I still really don't, why or how anyone could sleep in or stay home on a beautiful ball morning.

Finally, in ones or twos, the town kids begin to straggle in, not enough to choose sides, but enough to play workup. You need to know the rules of the game.

The number of players needed for a game of workup can range from seven or eight to infinity. There are three batters. As long as a batter doesn't make an out and the lead batter of the three makes it home, they continue "up to bat." The players in the field are numbered: the pitcher number one, first base two, second base three, shortstop four, third base five, and all outfielders are sequentially numbered in the order they arrive at the field.

If a batter flies out, he exchanges places with the fielder who caught the ball. Good players can stay at bat for a long time, but eventually they ground out, fly out, or are forced out at home and must move to the outfield.

If a batter grounds out or if he is the lead runner and doesn't make it home after the other two have batted, he moves to the outfield and becomes the highest numbered player. Everyone else moves up one place; the pitcher becomes a batter, the first baseman becomes the pitcher, the second baseman moves to first and so on.

It becomes closer to the start of school and more and more kids arrive to join the game. The numbering system in the outfield becomes too cumbersome. New players simply ask, "Who do I follow?" There are way too many players, but it's too late to choose up sides for a regular game. The outfield becomes packed with an unruly mob, fighting and pushing for each fly ball. Luckily, we are literally "saved by the bell" as the five-minute warning sounds and everyone runs for their classroom.

I gather up the bats and ball and rush after them.

The Playground

I sometimes drive past the elementary playground where my children attended school and watch the latest generation at play. I am somehow saddened by their times and their circumstances. I know that fun and adventure are being experienced and imaginations are at work, but on such a small scale and in such a sterile and stifling arena. Fifteen sections of kids at play in a small concrete and pea gravel prison. The well-meaning teachers wandering among the students remind me of guards. I think back to the playground of my youth.

As far as I remember, the playground at Madelia's school was never referred to as such; we went out to play in the "park." I guess to some knowledgeable adults it was Flanders Park. The Madelia grade school and high school were located near the south end of this large double-block area. On the front and west side of the buildings, open grassy lawns sloped down to the streets. Here we played marbles in early spring as we waited for the park to dry, but this area was usually left to the little kids and maybe the girls. I never really knew what became of the girls during the noon or recess breaks.

The park occupied the northern two-thirds of the grounds, at least until fourth grade when a new high school and gymnasium claimed part of our territory. The greatest effect of this building project was to take away the soccer field. This was not a big loss to me since soccer was only played by a small group of "older kids."

The primary fixtures of the park included a log cabin (now preserved at the Watonwan Historical Society museum), a never-used band shell, a World War I cannon, a playground set, a seldom-used tennis court, a water tower, and a municipal plant that seemed abandoned and whose function remained a complete mystery. Scattered throughout the park's numerous elm, ash, and maple trees were a handful of ball diamonds; a couple of them were so permanent they actually had backstops.

This was our domain. There were not a large number of us when one actually stops to count. Each elementary grade had one section of about twenty-five students. If you subtract the lower grade students, who spent most of their time in front or at the swing sets, those who had no interest in outdoor adventure, and the mysterious girls, you can see there was plenty of space for the rest of us.

Proprietorship of the ball fields had evolved a loosely structured hierarchy. Each class moved from year to year to the next most desirable location. Fifth and sixth graders controlled the prime, backstopped diamonds. Football and tackle tag fields were fitted into any open space that could be found and were bounded by, or dangerously close to, large immoveable trees.

The log cabin's primary function was to serve as an obstacle for any ball hit between second and third base. A sharp line drive hit down the third base line might slip past it into left field, and I suppose a fly ball could theoretically clear the cabin and reach the outfield, but the space above the cabin was well guarded by a dense canopy of elms. A glancing blow off the roof sometimes bounced over for a hit, but most deflections bounced backwards and were caught for outs.

What the cabin actually contained remained a mystery; its windows were boarded and the door kept securely locked.

We used the cannon and the band shell as backdrops for epic snowball battles. As far as I know, they were never used to shoot anyone or to hold musicians.

Flanders Park. The log cabin, the cannon and, behind it, the band shell. (Photo courtesy of the Watonwan County Historical Society)

I don't remember being explicitly told that the water tower was off limits, but everyone seemed to know this was the case. As a result of this suspected ruling, climbing was restricted to times when school was not in session, especially during the dark of night.

Once a year the trees emerged from their background role to participate in the activities. Each May the soft maple trees produced a much sought-after product. Seeds that would later in the year come spinning down like small helicopters now served as nature's squirt guns. When squeezed, a stream of fluid would shoot out of the base, making them excellent close combat weapons.

Not everyone participated in sports activities. Some kids congregated in nooks and crannies, where they played games of their own invention, or wandered through the park, going where their imaginations took them.

The park provided the backdrop of our youth. Each of us who played there has memories and perceptions of the activities that took place within its sidewalk boundaries. We selected our teams and decided who was out or who was safe. We policed our quarrels and settled our differences. We were sometimes bruised and broken, but there was no thought of lawsuits or of parents blaming the school or our teachers.

I don't remember teachers, or for that matter, any adult, ever invading our space. We grew up on our own terms.

The Bully

The only connection between Howard James and myself was that we were the smallest kids in our classes.

Howard was in junior high, three years ahead of me. For some reason, known only to him, he began to push me whenever we met or made threatening comments under his breath when we passed each other. I began watching for him, attempting to avoid him at all costs. He had achieved the goal of all bullies: I was terrified.

One noon, on the playground in front of the school, he began to chase me. I was a fast runner for my age, but Howard was just a little faster and gradually gained on me. Just as he was attempting to reach out and grab me, I dropped to the ground in a ball, tripping and sending him rolling across the ground. I was up and running in a flash, but Howard, now more determined than ever, began again cutting into my lead.

My newfound evasive maneuver was repeated again with the same result, except that now my pursuer was more embarrassed and angrier than ever. The third time was not a charm. Prepared for my trick, Howard screeched to a halt, landed on top of me, and came up sitting across my chest. I was doomed.

I don't know if you have ever seen the Disney cartoon character, the Tasmanian Devil. He is a spinning whirling dervish, able to terrorize the largest victim. My Tasmanian Devil appeared in the form of my brother Arlo, then in first or second grade. Out of the corner of my eye I saw him coming, running at top speed, a look of vengeance and determination in his eye. He crashed into Howard, sending him sprawling onto his side.

Being bested by a kid Arlo's size must have been more than his ego could handle; Howard got up and walked away.

A few days later I got up enough courage to tell my dad, "Howard James is always picking on me at school." Dad made many of his purchases at the James Brothers' hardware store, and Rich James, Howard's father, was a good friend of his.

Howard never bothered me again.

I never properly thanked Arlo or my dad for rescuing me. Thanks.

Rafts

Boys are attracted to water like rats to a dump. I had two sloughs. Two hundred yards south of our homestead was a cattail-encircled marsh that was divided into two parts by our township road. The same distance to the east, we had a larger, mostly open slough, more like a small muddy lake. I taught high school ecology for twenty-five years, but have never understood why the millions of cattail seeds that were blown each fall from the south slough to the east slough failed to sprout and grow.

The east slough was a quarter mile across and the one to the south slightly smaller. Both were about four feet deep, a depth that never seemed to vary. Dad told me that during the droughts of the 1930s, both had dried up and been farmed, but for me they remained loyal and reliable sources of recreation.

A sort of spiritual eminent domain left no doubt in my mind that the sloughs belonged to me. The County Recorder's Office held a slightly different view. Their records showed the south slough belonged to Wilbur Lindstrom and the east to Wilbur, Victor Christenson, and my father. But for rare occasions during duck hunting season, the sloughs were my exclusive property.

Mud bottoms and mud shores make muddy feet. I spent hours fooling around on the edges of these wetlands with my feet wholly or partially submerged in gooey slime. Mother kept a hose connected to an outside faucet where I was regularly sentenced to wash my bare feet or muddy shoes.

It's difficult to embark on real adventure until one is old enough to master the use of a hammer and saw. I was around ten when I first began pounding pieces of scrap lumber together in an attempt to sail, or at least float, the bounding main. A critical mass is needed to generate the buoyant force required to support a small boy. My crafts usually failed to meet this requirement and upon receiving my weight, promptly sank.

My fortunes changed one spring day. I came home from school to find Dad and our hired man, Herb, replacing a big door on our cattle barn. The old one, about twelve-by-fifteen feet, had been dropped in the yard, destined for the burn pile.

I went right to work. I managed to pick up one front corner and pull that side of the door a few feet forward. I dropped the corner and picked up the opposite side, duplicating my small advance. Two hundred yards is a long way, but over the course of several outings I zigzagged the door through the pasture to the east slough. I'm sure Dad and Herb had a good chuckle over the disappearance and transport of the door. At least my efforts kept me out of their hair.

Launching my craft was a little tricky and, of course, muddy. I had to wiggle it forward until the front end, and eventually the entire craft, began to float. All I needed now was a form of propulsion. Snooping around the farm, I found a long two-by-two board; it wasn't ideal but it was the best I could do.

It was time for her maiden voyage. I stepped aboard, jabbed the pole into the muddy shore, and shoved off. It floated. It more or less supported my weight. The problem was that when I stood near the stern to pole, that edge gradually sank and the raft began to tip precariously. The tipping was slow enough, however, that I could get in several good pushes before I had to step to the center and allow the craft to regain her equilibrium. The problem was minor when compared to the exhilaration of skimming across the slough. I was sailing.

People talk of vessels having a shallow draft. Mine may have set a world record: I could keep it afloat in three inches of water. What a summer of adventure. I was free to sail whenever I wanted, although a few times I had to retrieve my craft from the far side when she came loose from her moorings after a big storm. Surprisingly, my raft made a better two-man vessel than a single. A second crewmember, standing near the bow, balanced and stabilized the raft and eliminated the annoying "sinking stern" problem.

The wise sailor would have pulled his craft up and dry-docked her for the winter; by dumb luck mine was still sitting on our shore the following spring. The day was warm and the ice had melted, perfect weather for the first voyage of the year. I wiggled her free and cast off, jumping at the last second to avoid stepping in the cold water. I was immediately confronted with a strange meteorological phenomenon, one that I had not seen before and one I have never heard or read about since. The slough had frozen so deeply that winter that even though the water was its normal four feet deep, the bottom was still a sheet of solid slippery ice. My attempts at propelling the craft with the two-by-two were futile; the ice provided no resistance and the pole merely slipped across the bottom.

There had to be a solution. It was too nice a day to be grounded. I dug around in Dad's machine shed until I found the perfect tool: a fish spear. The spear was a wicked looking weapon; its business end held six long, barbed tines, designed for impaling large northern pike. The right tool for the job is critical. I jabbed the spear into the icy bottom and cruised around the slough in fine fashion.

A few days later I returned for another voyage. I eagerly shoved off but, much to my surprise, the bottom ice had melted and I was stranded away from shore with only my fish spear for a push pole. The recent advantages of this tool quickly turned into a liability; each time I pushed on the shaft, the tines sank into the soft bottom. When I tried to pull the spear out of the mud, the tines held fast and the raft moved backwards. The old "two steps forward, one step back" had been replaced by "one step forward, one step back." I was stranded.

Necessity being the mother of invention, I turned the spear around and held the tine end while pushing in the mud with the handle. The results were only slightly improved; the thin spear handle also tended to mire in the sticky bottom. I was slowly making my way back to shore when the shaft sunk deeply into the bottom and stuck. I gave the spear a quick pull, releasing it from the mud but ramming one of the muddy tines into my leg. Luckily it didn't enter deep enough for the barb to penetrate my limb. I made it to the shore and back to the house with my pants torn and my leg bleeding. I still have a scar on the inside of my thigh and a general idea of how Moby Dick must have felt.

The elements eventually claimed the raft. Romantically, I would like to think she broke up in a big gale. More likely she just rotted away.

More and improved rafts followed. I was now driven to develop crafts for my newfound obsession: duck hunting. The new rafts were built from abandoned telephone poles. Two long poles held together by a small platform and a few cross braces made a remarkably stable and manageable craft.

Fifty-gallon steel barrels, when cut along one of the long sides and down both ends, can be bent open to form a nifty two-chambered watercraft. With one foot in each compartment, it made a maneuverable boat that could be poled through the marsh to retrieve downed ducks or covered with cattails to make a floating blind. The major drawback of this design was its deep draft; when fully loaded with one medium-sized boy, the top edges were only a few inches above the waterline. If too much weight was placed on one side or the other, water would rush into the depressed compartment. A bailing can was standard equipment on a vessel of this design. Looking back, a life jacket wouldn't have been such a bad idea either.

None of these rafts were OSHA approved.

Snow

Everyone thinks the winters of his or her youth were the absolute worst. A few hits on Google can verify that in my case this was true. The winter of 1950 was, up until that time, the snowiest ever recorded for Minnesota. The situation was compounded, compared with today, by the size and quality of the snow removal equipment.

The biggest storms hit in February and March. Snow plowing provided a temporary solution but later increased the problem. Windblown snow covered the road and had to be pushed ever higher to keep the road open. Soon the snow banks were piled higher than our car. The inevitable day arrived when another big storm hit and the road cut was again filled to the top. The township snowplow made a valiant effort but, after repeatedly ramming the hardened drifts, was forced to turn away, damaged and defeated. We were marooned.

More storms came and the drift that had once been our road continued to grow. Our telephone poles ran along the side of the west ditch. Big blue-green insulators bolted to wooden crossbars supported the wires. I would stand on top of the drifts and listen as the chest-high wires vibrated in the wind, emitting an eerie humming buzz. I knew the phone wires weren't electrified but could never summon the courage to touch one and prove I was right.

It was two weeks before all of the state and county roads were opened, finally freeing the big equipment for use on the township roads. I stood with my nose against the window and watched a huge white geyser approach from the south. The big snow blower chewed and spit its way up our road, freeing us at last.

Except on days when there were actual blizzards, our school remained open, attended by those who lived in town and by the few country kids who could find a way to get to class. I was one of the unfortunates; my dad owned a team of horses.

The team of big sorrel Belgiums was hooked to the bobsled, Marlys and I loaded into the box, and we headed for town. We didn't take the township road; it was covered with ten-foot drifts. We traveled directly east across the fields and over the big slough. The snow was chest deep in some places and the team sweated and puffed as it lunged through the deepest drifts. From time to time Dad would pull them up and let them catch their breath. The going got easy once we reached Highway 15: the runners slid smoothly through the shallow snow on the road's shoulder.

We turned off the highway as soon as we reached town and took the street that passed my grandmother's house. As we neared the school we began to pass kids walking along the street, and Dad would stop the team and invite them aboard. By the time we reached school, our bobsled box was overflowing and some of the oldest kids were riding on the runners. It was the first time most of them had ridden in a big sled. I felt proud, as if I was at least partially responsible for their enjoyment.

One winter we visited my Uncle Frank and Aunt Florence's home in Hancock. The snow had filled their yard so deeply that the drifts had become an extension of their chicken house roof. Behind that structure, the older kids were working on an excavation project. Their plan was to dig all the way to the ground and then sideways to construct a hideout. My job was to stay out of the way. They hauled snow to the top in pails and dumped it off to one side. When the workers needed a break, they were pulled to the surface with a thick rope. I remember crawling forward on my stomach and peering over the edge, marveling at their amazing feat of engineering.

Dad cleaned out our yard after a big snowstorm and, using his tractor and loader, piled a huge mound of snow next to the gas pump. I worked for what seemed like hours digging a cave into one side of the pile. Progress was slow, my primitive tools and puny strength no match for the packed snow. Dad walked by on his way to the corncrib carrying a big aluminum scoop shovel. I don't remember him saying a word; he just stopped and began shoveling. Snow flew. In a couple of minutes I had a cave big enough to stand and walk around in. The room was very dark and quiet. It smelled like snow.

One year a strange late spring snowfall caught us by surprise. We came out of our house the morning after and found that our world had turned pink. A massive weather system had blown Oklahoma dust high into the atmosphere and snowflakes had formed around the red soil particles. The south side of the snow banks turned from pink to red as the snow melted, concentrating the dust particles. At least two amateur meteorologists, my mother and I, ever after referred to this as the "winter of the pink snow."

We were stir crazy. It seemed like the winter would never end. I suppose my father eventually grew tired of hearing us bellyache. Word was passed down that we were going to the movies.

We bundled up in our warmest clothes and headed out to the freezing car; no gas had been wasted warming it up. I sat in back and melted pictures on the frosted side window. The ditches were filled level with the road and windblown snow was drifting across, making the whole world look the same. It happened in slow motion: Dad, unable to see the road, drove into the ditch. We climbed out of the car and trudged back to the farm through the blowing snow.

I think back on the situation now and feel sorry for Dad. He hadn't wanted to go to the show in the first place and now his problems were multiplying. We were crying because we had been unfairly cheated out of seeing a movie, and while Mom was stoic, he could tell she was almost as disappointed as we were. Dad probably felt worse than anyone. Not only had he disappointed his family, in the morning he would have to hitch up the team, drive through the blowing snow, shovel around the stranded car, and pull it out of the ditch.

CROQUET

In the days before the invasion of European night crawlers, lawns were smooth. Families came out of their houses in the long evenings before the advent of television and played croquet. Our family took croquet more seriously than most. The only time our court was taken down was when the lawn was being mowed. The stakes and arches were reset as soon as the mower moved on.

One member of our family moved the playing of croquet far beyond serious and into the realm of fanaticism.

The first croquet game I remember watching was at my Uncle Frank and Aunt Florence's farm near Hancock, Minnesota. I remember the laughs and banter as the clusters of players moved around the lawn. All the participants held the handles of their mallets near the center or at the top except for one, my Cousin Sherwood. He grasped his just above the head of the mallet with his hands almost touching the ground and his posterior high in the air. When he shot he closely resembled a crab. Sherwood, three years older than me, was my idol and also a very good player. I naturally copied his style when I got big enough to begin playing.

I will describe the finer points of this shooting style. The top of the handle is placed tightly under the right armpit, and the left hand and then the right grasps at the very bottom, as close to the mallet head as possible. This combination provides a level of stability and accuracy impossible to achieve by any other method. The hands, being close to the contact point, provide a special touch to each shot, almost as if the ball was being thrown. The downside of this method is that it requires enduring the stares and comments of all onlookers. This spectacle increases with age as the player's legs continue to lengthen and the ground remains more or less in the same position.

I soon became old enough to join our evening games and I would hurry to the court after supper to claim the orange or yellow mallet. Everything proceeded normally for a couple of years until a problem developed. I became a fanatic. I began spending long hours practicing. At first I practiced as if I were playing golf, counting the strokes it took to complete the course and always attempting to improve my best score. Soon I began experimenting with shot technique and ball control.

I will explain a few rules of croquet. The object of the game is to become the first to circle the court while hitting your ball through an array of wire arches. A player may strike an opponent's ball with their own and be awarded three options: leave the opponent's ball where it lies and continue on with two bonus shots; place the two balls together, put your foot on your ball, and strike it firmly (your ball, not your foot), sending the opponent's ball flying down the court; or, lastly, align the two balls in close proximity to each other and strike your ball, sending both balls rolling simultaneously. In the last two scenarios the player has one free shot remaining.

The shooter's ball must pass through the next required arch before the same opponent may again be struck.

I worked to control the speed and direction of two balls rolling at the same time. I varied the distance and alignment between the two balls and experimented with different follow-through techniques. I could eventually make my back ball pass the front ball or could make the front ball run on ahead. I learned to make both balls stop exactly where I wanted them.

I refined my strategy. I would throw a phantom opponent's ball somewhere in front of the first arch, shoot my ball through and, with my next shot, hit the opponent's ball. With my first bonus shot I would align the two balls and strike my ball, sending the opponent's ball to the far side of the next arch and stopping mine on the front side. With my second bonus shot I would hit my ball through the arch. I now had a shot coming to me for passing through the arch and would use it to again strike the opponent's ball. I repeated this process, escorting the opponent's ball from arch to arch, until I had completed the entire course in one turn.

My success at this and other similar strategies resulted in creation of the "three strike rule." Under this system, I was only allowed to hit a total of three balls before I had to stop shooting and pass my turn on to the next player. This rule allowed our family to continue playing competitive games. It wasn't much fun for me or the other players if I hogged all the shots.

Bill Manahan, a friend and classmate of mine, was one of the best athletes to ever graduate from Madelia High School. I was shooting snooker in Vern's Pool Hall one summer evening when Bill made a rare appearance into that den of iniquity. I happened to mention that the only two sports I could beat him at were pool and croquet. I could see the competitive fire grow in his eyes as he expressed his doubt about the latter and challenged me to a croquet match.

We drove to his house and walked to his backyard where a court was set up. It was agreed that we would play a best out of ten series with a dollar awarded to the winner. I won six games in a row.

A few weeks later I was surprised to get a phone call from Bill. He wanted a rematch. I could only assume that he had been practicing and would be better prepared the second time around. I don't remember if there was another wager, but I do remember again winning six straight games. Our croquet competitions ended.

Croquet is no longer a common activity. The ubiquitous night crawlers have ruined our lawns, and television, computer games, and a hundred other activities now keep families from spending long summer evenings together. I will always remember the great fun we had. My parents were good players and my sister and brother were both excellent. Our contests were legendary.

I am aware there are people who still play croquet. They wear white shorts outfits, fancy wide-brimmed hats, and shoot the ball through sturdy wooden arches called wickets. They hold club, state, and national tournaments on strangely arranged, golf-green-like courts. At the end of these contests one player is declared champion.

I challenge their right to this title. I maintain that to truly by crowned champion, they must return in time to a certain sloping croquet court in Southern Minnesota, where they will find a young boy waiting. I am not saying that none can beat him, but, if they do, I suspect they will choose orange or yellow and shoot the ball from a strange crouched position closely resembling that of a crab.

The Roller Rink

All of the radios in our house were tuned to one station: WCCO. We received our national and regional news, grain and livestock market reports, sports, evening comedy and drama shows, and all our music from its airwaves. The station's musical programing, which took up at least half of their airtime, was primarily pop, show tunes, and Hit Parade favorites, not the scandalous rock and roll that was invading the airways at WDGY.

Roller skating arrived in Madelia one summer in the early 1950s. A large canvas tent was erected on the level ice skating rink along the north edge of the school park. A string of low-watt electric light bulbs, suspended beneath the outer support poles, kept the gray composite skating surface in semidarkness. At each corner of the rink, a speaker pointed inward, broadcasting announcements and playing what I thought of as "roller skating music."

I was no stranger to roller skating. I owned a pair of metal-wheeled clamp-on skates that I used to race around our basement furnace. In addition, my Uncle Ed had once taken me skating in New Ulm where I had polished my skills on the large National Guard Armory floor.

It was mid-July, nearing my twelfth birthday. My mother dropped me off around eight. The rink was bustling, the scrape and clack of skates blending with loud blaring music. I hurried up the ramp and rented and quickly put on my skates. Before I could make one circuit of the floor, the speaker announced, "Clear the floor, the next will be a couples only skate." I groaned and joined my friends on the wooden bench that surrounded the floor.

Many of the older couples were from out of town. They wore bright white skates with colorful tassels or pom-poms laced to the toes. The couples skated backwards, they twirled and dipped and kept perfect time to the music. They were a pain in the butt. I wanted to get back on the floor. Finally, after two or three songs, the announcement I had been waiting for arrived: "All skate."

My friends and I attacked the floor, skating at top speed, sliding out of control as we attempted to navigate the sharp turns. A warning from the speaker would temporarily slow our assault but, when we felt we had served our sentence, we would gradually resume our speed. The July night was hot and humid and soon we were flushed and sweating. The next time we were asked to clear the floor we didn't complain.

Moths and night bugs circled the lights and mosquitos slipped into the tent, attracted by the smell and heat of our sweating bodies. At ten o'clock, a time likely established by the city council, the speakers announced: "Last skate." I changed into my tennis shoes, returned the skates to the counter, and wandered into the night, looking to find where my mother had parked our car.

The years passed. From time to time, I would hear a song on a jukebox or on some obscure location on my radio dial and think, "That's a roller skating song." I now realize I had been listening to honky-tonk country music. Hank Williams, Webb Pierce, and Farren Young had carved an indelible mark in my receptive young mind.

In spite of WCCO's best efforts to shelter me from such low class music, I eventually became hooked on "roller skating" music. Last year I received two Hank Williams CDs for Christmas.

Marbles

Children have played marbles for generations. This time-honored sport contains a vast lexicon of terminology: knuckle down, fudging, rollsies, spannies, and throwsies, to list a few. The vast array of marble types include glassies, smokies, peeries, commies, aggies, and steeleys. There are many standardized games. The most common is ringer, a game in which a shooter marble is flicked off the forefinger with the thumb in an attempt to knock marbles out of a circle or ring. This was the game my father played when he was a boy.

None of this great marble tradition survived, or maybe ever reached, the playing fields of my youth. Our contests had devolved to a degraded form, the pageantry of the game's heyday long forgotten. The marble season was short, played each year during that brief period between the end of winter and the day the tackle tag and softball fields became dry enough for use.

We played marbles on the lawns that sloped south and west from the school. The term "lawn" here is loosely used to describe the hard-packed, footprint-trampled landscape between the school and the sidewalks. Our competitions consisted of two simple games: dabs and pots.

Dabs was a game for two contestants. The first player would "cast out," throwing his shooter some distance in front of him. The second player, standing in the same place, would then throw his shooter, attempting to hit the first player's marble. The trick was to throw your shooter hard enough so it would roll past the object marble and not be an easy target for your opponent should you miss. Turns were exchanged until one player hit the opponent's shooter. Since we always played marbles "for keeps," the loser was required to give the winner a marble from his bag.

Pots was the big money game, played for "all the marbles." A hole a few inches across was kicked into the ground with the heel of a shoe. Each contestant dropped one marble into the pot and moved behind a line that had been scratched in the dirt. In turn, each contestant attempted to throw his shooter into the pot. The one who stopped his shooter closest to the pot was the winner. If two or more succeeded in landing in the pot, only these contestants would continue throwing until there was one winner. A big game of pots might involve ten or more players. The excitement of a large, multiple-tie game often attracted large crowds of onlookers. Pots was a boom or bust game. Your odds of winning were lower than with dabs, but if you were hot or having a lucky day, your marble bag could fatten considerably in one noon's session.

In sixth grade I was a member of the School Patrol. I always attempted to serve my noon duty at the high-traffic, southwest corner where all the kids passed on their way "up town," rather than at the boring Catholic Church corner where few students crossed.

Naturally, during the marble season I maintained a deep smooth pot close to my corner, between the sidewalk and the curb. I suspect there may have been times when the excitement of the contest sacrificed the safety of my clients.

I remember one particular day when I forgot my marble bag in the classroom. A group of players soon stopped, expecting a game. I dug around and found a colored gumball in my pocket and slyly slipped it into the pot in place of a marble. Borrowing a marble to use as a shooter, I threw and won the pot. By the time the bell rang, I had acquired a large pocketful of marbles. I now realize if I had lost that first pot and my deception been discovered, I would certainly have had my thumbs broken.

I wasn't the best player, but by the time I entered seventh grade and became too cool to play children's games, I was in possession of a two-pound coffee can full of marbles.

Taken For A Ride

Summer evenings were long and peaceful. Dad, finished with a hard day of work, dabbled. He changed the oil in a tractor, mowed the lawn, or repaired broken machinery.

Mom worked in her gardens, where flowers held priority over vegetables. Herbicides were unheard of and, as hard as she tried, she never quite managed to stay ahead of the weeds.

I was busy as well. There were stick horses that needed training, castles to be built in the sand box, and all sorts of monsters and bad guys to be hunted down with slingshots, rubber band guns, or my trusty Red Ryder BB gun. Sloughs had to be checked, trees climbed, and kittens in the haymow tamed.

The entire family would often gather on the lawn at dusk and play croquet. The evening ended when it became too dark to see or we were driven indoors by mosquitoes.

Occasionally there would be a change in our routine. An hour or so before dark, Dad would suddenly ask, "Who wants to go for a ride?" We all did. Mar and I pulled the seats forward and climbed in back, and Arlo rode up front between our parents. Although Dad was the captain, it seemed as if the car was rudderless. We slowly wandered along the country roads with our windows down, our path seemingly aimless. We might sight the Lake Crystal water tower or suddenly cruise through the main street of Hanska. We sometimes drove past farms that Dad managed for his brothers or checked out an area that had been struck by hail. Dad most of all enjoyed looking at the crops, seeing how they compared with his own.

No matter the direction or route taken, the car, with an uncanny sense of direction and timing, managed to arrive at the Madelia drive-in just as darkness settled across the countryside. The excruciating selection of treats was usually settled in favor of a root beer float. Mom and Dad always seemed to know the people in the cars on either side. While they carried on two- or three-way conversations, we stirred, sucked, and spooned the contents from our dripping frosty mugs.

We placed the empty mugs and soaked paper napkins on the tray, buzzed for the carhop, and drove the short distance home. Exhausted, we climbed to our rooms and stumbled into bed. Mom and Dad turned on the radio and listened to Cedric Adams' ten o'clock news and followed us up the steps.

STATE FAIR

The Minnesota State Fair typically has more than a hundred thousand visitors each day. I contributed to that total the summers before my fifth and sixth grades. Darwyn Johnson's father owned a camper, and Darwyn invited me to attend the fair with his family. I slept over at Darwyn's and we left for St. Paul at the first hint of daylight. Parking was on a first come, first served basis.

The fair board had set aside a fenced-in area along Snelling Avenue where families could set up tents or hook up their camping vehicles. Access between the campground and the fairgrounds was through a tall, narrow, turnstile-guarded gate. The turnstile was opened at daybreak and allowed to turn freely until eleven at night, when it was padlocked and rendered immovable until the following morning.

We arrived at the camp area before nine. Darwyn's mom and dad began setting up and organizing the camper, and Darwyn and I were turned loose, warned to be back at noon for dinner. This was our second year at the fair so we had a general idea of its layout. Darwyn was a town kid. I would have preferred to begin at the livestock barns, but these were far down his list of preferred attractions. We headed directly to the grandstand.

Darwyn loved cars. In the concourse beneath the seating area, American automobile companies displayed their latest concept vehicles, usually small, low convertibles sporting the latest in fins and chrome. Early in the day, before the crowds gathered, we could get close to the ropes and view the cars at our leisure. My favorite was a shiny blue Buick Wildcat. This futuristic beauty, while never manufactured for sale, became the namesake for later Buick models.

Our next stop was Machinery Hill, a three-block area packed with the latest in farm machinery. The displays were sponsored by big equipment manufacturers or by local Minnesota dealers. I gravitated toward the J. I. Case lot. My uncles, Carl and Ed, owned a Case dealership and this was the only brand of equipment used on our farm. No one tried to sell us any machinery; our only communication with the salesmen came in the form of a directive: "Hey you kids, get off that tractor."

We wandered down to the Midway and watched the workers prepare for the eleven o'clock opening. Workers, many wearing the same dirty clothes as last week, greased gears and warmed up engines. Rides were put though last minute checks and trial runs. Hawkers removed canvas fronts from their stands and straightened and organized their props and prizes. Several, open for business, sweet-talked and cajoled, attempting to draw in the few available marks. Some of those present, having had considerable experience in losing money at their county fair, politely resisted the advances; besides, it was time for dinner.

Mrs. Johnson had packed a basket the night before; our picnic table was filled with sandwiches, fruit, cookies, and a large pitcher of Kool-Aid.

"Don't forget to be back at six o'clock for supper."

We didn't have time to waste eating; it was almost time for the stock car races. Our tickets had been purchased earlier when we visited the grandstand. We joined a long line and shuffled our way up the big central ramp and located our seats. I didn't know much about automobile racing but Darwyn's enthusiasm was catching. The cars raced in several heats, the top drivers in each qualifying for the big feature race at the end of the program. The cars roared around the packed dirt oval, skidding in the turns and throwing dirt on the other contestants and into the lower rows of the spectators. I was soon bored.

Happy when the races were finally over, I guided Darwyn toward the barns. Beef cattle, sheep, swine, and poultry, we checked out all the buildings. Darwyn didn't lose interest; he had never had any. Only the mammoth-sized Budweiser six-horse team caught his attention. Handlers were leading the Clydesdales from their stalls as we passed. We shrank against the wall, anxious to avoid their dinner-plate-sized hooves.

The streets and venues were packed with hot, sweating fairgoers. Moving and dodging through the milling mass became a monumental task. We drank all the milk we could for a dime and sipped malts in the dairy building, watching as Princess Kay of the Milky Way was sculpted in butter. We ate caramel corn and mustard-coated Pronto Pups and wandered through the unending exhibit halls. Rural families, with long distances ahead of them, departed, replaced by city people, hurrying to the fair after work.

Our favorite game was the Rabbit Run, one of the few where skill outweighed chance. We each selected one of eight stools. In front of each participant was a box with a wooden lever and three numbered, ever-smaller holes. We handed over our dime and sat poised, waiting for the bell to ring. At its signal, we pushed down the lever, attempting to throw a rubber ball through one of the holes. Whether we were successful or not, the ball rolled back in place, ready to be launched again. A fifteen-foot racetrack extended forward and upward from the boxes. A ball that entered the smallest hole moved a mechanical rabbit ahead three spaces on the track, the next larger hole, two, and the largest, a single space.

"And they're off." The operator announced the race through a loudspeaker, adding excitement to the race as well as, hopefully, drawing prospective customers to his venue. If you knew your rabbit's number, you could know its position in the race without looking up. The first rabbit to reach the finish line triggered a loud bell, signaling the end of the race and earning the winner a coupon good for a small prize. The largest prizes, giant stuffed animals, required a pocketful of coupons. We stopped and played a few games each time we passed the stand. The practice gained from repetition helped us win a large percentage of the games and to add to our collection of coupons.

The late August afternoon sun grew ever hotter and our pace began to drag. We returned for supper a little early, not hungry, but happy to sit in the shade and rest.

Night brought a special magic. The Midway seemed a different place, alive with bright lights and a hint of danger. The air was still and sultry and the streets radiated the day's stored heat. Boys with girls on their arms and men with deep pockets threw around money, determined to win a teddy bear or best each other in manly contests.

I can't remember all the ways we spent our money and time, although I know we had much more of the latter. We rode the "World's Tallest Ferris Wheel," hoping it would stop when we were at the top. We listened to pitches for sword swallowers, bearded ladies, contortionists, and two-headed cows.

We watched men shoot at moving targets, attempt to ring a bell with a sledgehammer, and waste money attempting to tip over lead milk bottles.

We joined a large crowd of mixed-age men in front of the Club Lido. Two nearly-young ladies, dressed in high heels and risqué two-piece outfits, adorned the stage, standing, turning, or parading as instructed. A slick-looking mustachioed barker waved his thin cane and extolled the beauty of the ladies, hinting at their dancing prowess and at the even more beautiful women waiting inside.

It was nearly showtime. The dancers walked through a curtained door. A stream of hopeful men handed over dollar bills and followed.

We weren't sure what the men expected to see, but suspected that, much as we had earlier when paying good money to see the snake women and the freak show, they were about to be sorely disappointed.

The crowd began to thin and finally fade away. Workers shut down the machines and closed up their stands. Cleanup crews emerged and began sweeping and washing down the littered, grease-coated streets and sidewalks. We walked up the hill and past the Rabbit Run. For some reason, this was the last open stand in the fairgrounds. The operator, now our friend, allowed the game to go on as long as there were four or more players. Soon we were the only two.

Darwyn and I scaled the projecting arms of the turnstile and squeezed through a kid-sized space at the top. We tiptoed into the camper, crawled into our beds, and were immediately asleep.

Tomorrow would be a long day.

Saturday Night

My earliest memories of Saturday nights are of seas of legs. My sister Marlys is leading the way as we twist and turn down the crowded sidewalk, attempting to navigate the long double block between Adolf's grocery store and the movie theatre. We each clutch a quarter. Twelve cents is reserved for the cost of admission, and the remainder is ours to spend.

The movie usually seemed to star Randolph Scott. Randolph, while prolific, was vanilla compared to Roy Rogers or Gene Autry. Even his dark, drab, nameless horse was vanilla.

Marlys and I squeeze our change and stare into the glass case. We eventually agree on an acceptable combination of popcorn and candy, hand our tickets to Mr. Larkin, and grope down the dark aisle.

Americans had recently passed through two long and difficult trials: the Great Depression, followed by the Second World War. Automobiles were worn out. Most people hadn't been able to afford a new car during the Depression and cars weren't manufactured during the war. All industrial production had been directed to the war effort. The great automobile companies of Detroit had spent four years churning out Jeeps, tanks, trucks, airplanes, and other military vehicles.

Many of my early childhood memories coincide with the post-war recovery. Gasoline and certain kinds of food continued to be rationed. Millions of people throughout Europe and Asia were starving following the absolute destruction of their cities and their economies. America continued to export massive quantities of food and supplies to both our allies and our former enemies in an effort to prevent the collapse of their governments and societies.

The people of Madelia and every other small community shopped locally; no one was about to waste gasoline driving to another town or give their money to some outsider. Madelia's businessmen, sometime in the distant past, had made the decision to keep their stores open on Saturday nights. This commitment evolved into a partnership-like relationship between the storeowners and a certain segment of the area's rural population. My family was firmly in that group.

I don't know that we actually went to town every Saturday night, but in my mind we did. Dad would make a conscious effort to finish his fieldwork and livestock chores a little early so that by six thirty we could be on our way to Madelia. Adolf Larson's small grocery store, tucked in the back of Larson's department store, was accessible from Buck Street, the only street that led north from Madelia's shopping district.

Our Saturday nights were centered on Adolf's store. Dad would drop us off in front and look for a parking spot. Mom, after giving us a time to meet back at the store, would hand her weekly grocery list to Adolf and head out to complete the rest of her shopping.

Adolf was missing one arm; the lower half of his shirtsleeve was neatly rolled and safety pinned a short distance above his missing elbow. The loss of an appendage appeared to be no handicap; he would take Mother's list and systematically gather each item, placing it in a paper bag on the counter. I was no stranger at watching Adolf work. His little store was a home away from home. It was from here that Marlys and I phoned home and where we waited for our parents after any daytime school or community activity. If we needed money, we asked Adolf and he added the amount to Mother's monthly bill. He would even allow us to search for rare coins in his cash register if the store wasn't busy.

I gradually expanded the range of my Saturday night explorations, radiating from Adolf's much like a young animal explores outward from the safety of its den.

The closest point of excitement was a short distance away, at the corner of Buck and Main. On warm summer nights, the popcorn wagon and drinking fountain at that intersection were the center of the universe. Sooner or later, everyone stopped for one or both of its offerings.

The popcorn corner was poorly policed and a place the undisciplined could get themselves into many forms of difficulty. Popcorn could be thrown and water spit, squirted, sprayed, or loaded into balloons. Under extreme situations, vigilantes rose up and took the law into their own hands.

Main Street was well lit, but the side streets and especially the surrounding alleys were dark and forbidding. I remember the thrill and excitement when, accompanied by an equally timid friend, I summoned the courage to navigate the long, two-block alley behind Adolf's, eventually emerging at the far end and returning to the bright lights of Main Street.

The south side of Main Street held a strange double door that seemed to lead nowhere. The door was recessed into a brick wall and had no windows and no sign showing its function. We stood and stared. "I bet you don't dare." I looked both ways, opened the door a tiny crack, and peeked in. A wide row of steps led upward, disappearing into darkness. Here was excitement. "I'll go if you will." We crept in, tiptoed up the creaking steps, and waited for the loud scream or crashing monster we were sure would come. Nothing. We reached a small landing at the top and turned and looked at each other in the dim light, hearts pounding. We raced down the steps two at a time to the safety of the street.

The next Saturday we were back. The same caution and the same excitement. Three doors led from the upper landing. Two were locked, but the third, straight ahead, stuck, then broke free and swung open. A long row of wooden steps extended down to the alley below. We again turned and made a swift retreat to Main Street.

We understood the challenge. After a quick trip to the water fountain to steady our nerves and replenish our courage, we returned to the door. The plan was unspoken. We opened the lower door, raced loudly up the steps, through the door, and down the old wooden fire escape to the back alley. We stopped at a safe distance and looked back; the door was standing wide open. No one volunteered to return and close it.

Several of us were complicit in reinforcing the old adage, "Insanity is doing the same thing over and over and expecting different results." Every few weeks I was instructed to waste part of my Saturday night getting a haircut. Medieval-looking stone steps descended darkly from Main Street, past Ernie Jensen's subterranean barbershop, and back to ground level in the alley beyond. You didn't have to enter the packed room at the bottom; you only had to stick your head in the door, take a numbered card from a hook next to the doorframe, and wait for Ernie or his assistant Bob to tell you what number was presently in the chair.

Accurate calculations were required; you had to be in the shop when your number was called or you lost your place. How much playing and running around could you do before confining yourself to one of Ernie's boring waiting chairs? Every so often I would stick my head in the door and check where I was at. You had to ask; you couldn't tell by counting the number of people in the shop because a lot of old guys hung around and talked after they were finished.

It was too late to take chances. I entered and found a chair along the wall, picked up and discarded a shiny, boring *Esquire* and stared for the thousandth time at the framed word puzzle hanging on one wall. "Seville, der dago. Tausen busis inaro. Nojo demis trux. Summit cowsin summit dux." I had long ago deciphered the message but never failed to be mesmerized by its construction. "See Willie, there they go. Thousand buses in a row. No Joe, them is trucks. Some with cows and some with ducks."

The air hung heavy with the smell of Ernie's tonics and aftershave lotions. After an eternity, my number was called.

It didn't matter which chair I sat in because Ernie and Bob only knew one haircut. My hair was, and still is, extra fine and extra straight. Nothing short of glue could possibly alter its natural orientation. I cared nothing about appearance; it was speed that was important.

My stylist for the evening was more than willing to oblige my wishes. My hair was quickly shortened, the back of my neck shaved, a smelly fluid rubbed into my scalp, and my forclock combed neatly back. With a quick shake and snap of the barber cape, I was free.

The fact that my hairstyle remained perpetually unchanged remains a mystery. The front was cut diagonally across my forehead, evidently designed to fall in place when combed up and back. The plan always fell apart as soon as my hair dried and the lock descended to its preferred vertical position. I was doomed, but apparently contented, to travel through my childhood years with a pointy vampire-like forelock.

The pioneers had selected an excellent site to build the village of Madelia. The town was situated on a high terrace overlooking the Watonwan River, with its main street oriented in an east and west direction. There was just enough space for a narrow alley between the back of the buildings that lined the south side of Main Street and the terrace that sloped sharply down to a second level.

I'm not proud of a certain event that occurred along the edge of that terrace one Saturday night the summer before I entered sixth grade. I was walking through the alley with a couple of friends when we came across an old car with no wheels, sitting up on blocks. We gave the car a little push and it wiggled. That was strange; cars are really heavy. We gave it a stronger push and could almost feel it move. Wouldn't it be funny if we pushed the car off its blocks? We returned to Main Street and recruited two accomplices.

We lined up along the car and pushed in unison. Gravity and the laws of physics are mysterious things. The car didn't slide off the blocks as expected; instead, the blocks and automobile tilted as one unit, tipping the car on its side. Things were rapidly getting out of hand. The car, now fueled by momentum, wasn't content to remain on its side. The last thing I saw as I raced down the alley with adrenaline-induced panic was a rolling car and, far below, a house.

Saturday nights usually ended at ten. Dad would emerge from Joe's Garage across the street or from wherever he had been talking with friends, and Mom would return to Adolf's with her bags and packages. I would walk slowly past the long row of transparent, acetate-covered cookie boxes and make one last futile attempt to convince Mother the contents constituted one of the necessary food groups. That failed, we carried our supplies to the car and drove home.

Trapping

My neighbor, Alvin Spiess, was a renaissance man. He seemed able to do or fix anything. Back then people were allowed to throw anything into an open dump. Every few weeks the accumulated junk would be buried and covered over with a bulldozer.

Alvin would search for treasure, sometimes taking me along. There was absolutely no way of knowing what we might find. Some things could be salvaged and sold, some taken home and put to use, but most were just interesting and entertaining. Damaged or broken items made no difference to Alvin; he could fix anything. He could repair motors, restore electronics, and fix furniture. He could weld, solder, and glue. He brought home a bunch of discarded telephones and ran phone lines between all his outbuildings so us kids could call each other while we played. One day he brought home a broken guitar. He had never played a guitar in his life, but in a few minutes he had it repaired and was attempting to play along with a song on the radio. By the time the song ended, he had figured out the basics of guitar playing.

Alvin's farm was only eighty acres, much of it pasture. To supplement his income he trapped and, like everything else, he was good at it. He trapped muskrat, raccoon, and mink. Some Saturdays he would take me with him.

His trap line was forty or fifty miles long and included almost that many stops. I could never figure out how he remembered all the places he had to stop and once there, find the five or ten hidden sets at each site. His traps were placed along streams, rivers, and marshes. They were hidden in tiles and culverts and next to bridges, stumps, old pails, and objects projecting out of the water. He found faint trails I couldn't see and, if there were no trails, he still knew where the animals would step.

We would return to his farm late in the afternoon, his trunk filled with animals. On good days he worked late into the evening skinning, scraping, stretching, and hanging his pelts to dry. I tried to learn it all.

I was in sixth grade the fall I began trapping. I boiled my traps in walnut hulls to remove the shine and hide all human scent, and then hung them on the silo in anticipation of opening day. Wearing thick gloves, I loaded my traps in a five-gallon pail and headed for the slough. The road bank south of our farm was filled with old rocks and chunks of cement, placed as a barrier against erosion. Halfway between the water and the road surface, under a cement slab, I found a small hole. It looked like it was being used, but for what I didn't know. Contrary to everything I had learned from Alvin, I made a land set. Instead of placing the trap underwater to hide my scent, I carefully concealed it at the grassy entrance.

The next morning I was up in the cold morning darkness; traps could be checked any time after six o'clock. I could hear something. Twisting, half wrapped in the tall grass, was a large, dark mink, its eyes shining green in my flashlight. My hands shaking, I aimed carefully and shot him with my Marlin 22. He gave off a strong musk smell but he was beautiful; his fur was a smooth, shiny black and under his chin was a small patch of white.

I couldn't wait for Alvin to come home from his trap line so I could show it to him. Alvin skinned and stretched my mink and later, two others I miraculously managed to catch. When he sold his mink that winter he took me along and made sure I received top prices for my pelts. He showed up at our farm on Christmas Day with several handmade wooden stretching boards. Next year I would be expected to skin and stretch my catch.

Today I look at the Remington Wingmaster shotgun I purchased with the money I received for those three mink. It is aged and worn, much like its owner.

I continued to trap as long as I lived at home. One year I matched Alvin mink for mink for the first few weeks of the season, finishing the season with seventeen.

Mink were by far the most valuable pelts, but I also trapped raccoon, muskrats, and occasionally a skunk by accident. The first skunk I caught, I shot while standing downwind. My mother made me bury my clothes.

Winter arrived some years on a cold, calm night and the ice froze clear as glass. As soon as it was thick enough to support my weight, it was time to go muskrat hunting. I don't know if it was legal, but I would approach a muskrat house and kick or tap it with the side of my axe. The rats would burst out through an underwater tunnel and head for a safer house, their backs skimming along just under the smooth ice, a stream of bubbles marking their trail. Shuffling along in my overshoes, I would whack the ice above the rodent, stunning him, then chop a small hole and extract my prize. A good day might get me ten or twenty rats.

My father told me that in 1915, he and his brothers killed so many muskrats on our sloughs that they had to get a team and bobsled to haul them home. I recently found a photo, taken by my Uncle John, documenting this event. The muskrats were piled in a large mound next to the bobsled. I like the feeling of being connected to my past.

FOOTBALL

I dropped my Schwinn on its side and walked into the kitchen. Mom was sitting on a chair with a big enamel bowl in her lap, peeling potatoes.

"I'm one of the six best football players in my grade."

"Who told you that?"

As well as being skeptical, Mom hated bragging.

It had been decided that two football games would to be played the next day during recess. Bill Manahan, Dick Blue, and, I think, Conrad Keech would take on all the fifth-grade boys, and Billy Etter, Gary Blickem, and I, the entire fourth grade.

Three against twelve seemed about right. Gary and Billy were the biggest kids in our sixth grade.

Ours was not a passing attack; we took turns carrying the ball. Billy and Gary plunged straight ahead, fourth graders clinging to their legs like cockleburs. I ran around end or crashed into their ranks at top speed, using my head as a battering ram.

Both of our teams won their games. The results had to be reported as tactfully as possible.

Mom hated bragging.

Monkey Bars

In an attempt to solve the age old question as to which holds the most influence in our development, nature or nurture, I will put forward exhibit A: my shirt sleeves. I maintain that I can trace my lifelong difficulty in locating shirts to accommodate my thirty-five-inch arms to a single playground activity: the monkey bar wars.

Those of us who have lived through the post-9/11 era have seen videos of long lines of Al-Qaeda fighters swinging along on ladders as they trained to battle the infidels. Our ladder was similar to theirs but our intentions far less sinister.

It was a simple two-man game. Participants would start at opposite ends of the ladder and brazenly swing toward the center, eager to engage his opponent in combat. The object of the game was to swing your legs up, grasp the enemy firmly around the waist, and squeeze. Keep squeezing until he lets go his handhold and drops to the ground, and victory is yours.

I may have disrespected the integrity of the contest; while simple in concept, mastery required strategy, coordination, strength, and experience.

Follow me into battle. I swing out, watching the rhythm of my opponent, attempting to time my forward swing and catch him in a helpless position with his legs trailing behind. A quick squeeze and kill.

Victorious, I hang near the center of the ladder and wait. Soon, a new opponent swings out to meet me. I raise my legs as high as I can and quickly rush forward, making sure to keep my legs higher than his. A quick drop to his to waist and the squeeze. He is stubborn and refuses to drop. I move closer and transfer my weight to his body; eventually he surrenders.

I hold on alternately with one arm and then the other, trying to save strength. If the opponent is slow in arriving, I hook my legs on a bar above and hang upside down while I wait.

The wave of challengers is unending. Eventually, one highly skilled and well rested competitor swings out to meet me. I battle but make a mistake. A scissors clamp, and my fate is sealed.

I drop to the ground and move quickly to the end of one of the lines, hoping for a chance to restore my honor before the bell rings.

Mistaken Identity

I applied for my first passport in the 1990s and found, much to my astonishment, that I did not exist. No person named Wayne Feder had ever been recorded at the Watonwan County Courthouse. On July twenty-fourth, 1940, a boy named Feder had been born to Ervin and Hilda Feder. What a coincidence; I was born on the same date to the same parents.

I remember my mother telling me that she and Dad couldn't decide on a name for me. Finally, disgusted with their procrastination, my Uncle John came over to our farm and told my parents they had waited long enough and named me Wayne. Evidently the officials at the courthouse were never notified and only my legal name, Feder, remained on the books. I feel it important to point out in defense of my manliness that I was never listed as "Baby Boy Feder."

The reason for providing this information is to point out a marvelous opportunity lost. My elementary teachers were insistent that our complete and exact first and last names be attached to our work. In the few instances I signed with one or the other I was quickly reprimanded.

If only I had known. I can see the humiliation and embarrassment on their faces as I unfold my birth certificate and reveal my true identity.

"From now on, I'll be signing my papers 'Feder.'"

The Incident

The room was cavernous. Black-framed desks with stained, obsolete inkwell holes stood row on row. A raised platform at the front held a large solid oak teacher's desk, its only fixture a silver bell, similar to those found on store or motel counters.

I counted forward from the back; my assigned desk was near the window side of the room, three-fourths of the way down the row. Students from grades seven through twelve continued filing in, placing their books in stacks between their feet or in the hinged storage compartments below their desktops.

It was early in the fall of my seventh-grade year. Everything about my new building seemed strange and intimidating, especially the large mixed-age study hall. The squirming, organizing, and whispering quickly diminished when the hall bell rang, and stopped completely when Miss Randall, our high school principal, entered the room.

Broad and stern, Miss Randall mounted the steps, placed her work on the desk, took out her seating chart, and began taking attendance. That completed, she began working on administrative paperwork. We were expected to work as well. At the faintest whisper, Miss Randall would reach forward, pound three or four times on her bell, and quell the disturbance with a withering stare.

One deathly quiet day while I was reading a book it happened. Without warning, I let out a loud fart. As one, everyone in my field of vision turned and looked toward the source. My immediate response was to turn and look back with them. Of course everyone behind me was looking forward, directly into my now-red face.

Order was quickly restored with a few pounds on the bell.

A Short Vacation

Spring had come early. The leaves and wildflowers had exploded with the warm nights and sunny skies. It would be cruel to force kids to remain in school in such fine weather.

Virgil Boelter lived a mile east of town along Highway 60. A large woodlot, owned by some or other Feder, was located a short distance across the railroad track from his house and abutting the north shore of Fedge Lake.

Secret plans involving stick matches, raided cupboards, and borrowed cooking utensils were carefully laid. Our normal morning route was diverted toward Fedge, our bikes dragged across the tracks and hidden in a clump of dogwoods. We walked deep into the woods and, in the shelter of a wide-arching basswood tree, built a stick lean-to to serve as a home base for the day's activities and a small fire to dry our dew-soaked pants.

The woods, several football fields square, was new to us and required exploration. White patches of bloodroots and rue anemone dotted the forest floor and the smell of plum blossoms filled the air. Along the lakeshore, new-grown cattail stems thrust upward through last year's matted stalks.

Ducks circled and swooped, skidding on splayed webs to join the feeding flocks on the water. Bluebills and rust-headed canvasbacks arched above the water and disappeared in bill-first dives, popping to the surface holding long strands of pondweed. Pintail and teal tipped and bobbed, probing for crustaceans with their sensitive bills.

Mallards, the hens with blue wing patches and the drakes displaying impossibly green heads, drifted in and out along the edge of the cattails. We tied jackknives to straight willow sticks and stalked, first on our hands and knees and then on our bellies. It seemed we could reach out and touch them. They flew away.

We ate beans from a scorched kettle and chewed our fire-blackened hotdogs.

Our enthusiasm began to wane as the sun passed its zenith and our thoughts shifted toward tomorrow. Strategies, Virgil's mostly more honorable than mine, were discussed and discarded or shelved.

The afternoon dragged. With our final plan in place, every man for himself, we retrieved our bikes and headed home. I skirted town, careful to avoid classmate contact, and coasted into our yard at my normal time.

The next morning, I came down for breakfast in the middle of Dallas Townsend's *World News Roundup*. Looking back, I suppose my plan was rather weak: maybe my seventh-grade homeroom teacher would forget to ask for a note.

The phone rang. It was Mrs. Boelter. Virgil's plan had been more straightforward: he had simply told his mother what had happened.

It was times like these I appreciated having such a wise mom. "I'm not going to do anything this time, but don't ever let it happen again."

I never did.

My long-suffering mother with Marlys, Arlo, and me.

THE BALL GAME

I was twelve the summer I saw my first baseball game. I was visiting my Aunt Helen and Uncle Bob near Hancock, in west central Minnesota. Richie, Bobby, and Arlie all played on the town team for the tiny community of Danvers.

It was a home game. Shortly after supper, I climbed into the backseat of their family sedan with Richie and Bobby. They were wearing real baseball uniforms. Arlie met us at the field; he lived on a nearby farm with his young wife, Evie.

The small stadium and ballpark were bustling; the opposing team, Chokio, population four hundred, was taking batting practice. The players yelled and joked as they stood around the cage. After a short warm-up and a few swings, Danvers took the field, Arlie at first, Richie in the outfield, and Bobby behind the plate.

We found seats a few rows up, behind the wire backstop. I remember how the ball popped when it hit Bobby's mitt or cracked when it made contact with the bat. Everything looked fast and dangerous. The players on the field and in the dugouts kept up a constant chatter, encouraging their own and disparaging their obviously inferior opponents.

Groups of kids lined the outer fences, rushing mob-like through the parked cars to capture each foul ball and claim its ten-cent reward.

Each time one of my cousins came to bat I hoped for a home run or at least a hit.

The game crept on and the air cooled as the June sun sank below the horizon. I was freezing in my thin t-shirt.

Evie reached forward, wrapped a worn blanket around my shoulders, and pulled me close, holding me for the last two innings in a warm hug. It was wonderful.

People didn't hug at my house.

WHITETAIL

My neighbor, Curtis Lindstrom, was seven years older than me. I occasionally talked to him when I was hunting on his family's marsh near our farm. I received a new Marlin bolt-action 22 rifle for the Christmas the year I was twelve, and Curt offered to take me cottontail hunting. Dad was against my hunting with other kids but allowed me to go with Curt because of his age.

Curt picked me up on a cold January day and we drove a mile west to Wilson's Woods. We hunted north through the soft snow of the grazed, open woodland until we came to a four-strand barbed wire fence. Beyond, the forest changed abruptly. We had reached the path of the tornado and its shrubby new-growth forest. Thirteen years earlier, the year before I was born, a storm had flattened this section of woods before continuing westward and destroying much of our farm.

Curt held our rifles while I squeezed through the dangerous wire, then passed them to me and crossed to my side. Here was real cottontail country. We walked slowly, watching. Curt's hand was on my shoulder and he slowly pointed through the brush. I couldn't see what he was looking at. "Deer," he whispered.

I saw them: gray horizontal lines frozen against the vertical of the trees and shrubs, a small set of antlers, white muzzles, and the broken mass of their bodies.

Whitetail deer never were prairie animals; the few that had lived in the scattered woodlots and floodplain forests of Southern Minnesota were killed before my father's time. Agriculture practices, fire suppression, and windbreak plantings now favored the expansion of trees.

Ours were among the first deer seen in the Madelia area since the 1800s.

The deer watched us for a long time, frozen. The tension became too great and they broke, white flags flashing through the underbrush.

Ice Fishing

Wilson's Lake, a little over a mile northwest of our farm, was shallow and mud-bottomed, connected to the Watonwan River by Elm Creek. On the west side, a large drainage tile emptied into the lake.

Winter made survival difficult for the fish; the deeper the ice froze, the less space and oxygen remained. This problem was compounded in hard winters when deep snow blocked sunlight from penetrating the ice. Without light, aquatic plants were unable to photosynthesize and all available oxygen was quickly used up. The deepest, coldest days of January often triggered a crisis: the fish began to suffocate.

Salvation lay to the west. Warm oxygenated water, flowing from the drainage tile, maintained a small ice-free area along the edge of the lake, a sanctuary for the stressed fish.

Savvy fisherman checked the lake daily. Nothing. Suddenly they were there. They swarmed and they boiled. Young boys thought it possible to walk across the water on a carpet of fish.

Word spread, fishermen attracted by fish. No rods, no hooks, no spears; the only gear needed was a multi-tined silage fork. Hip boots in place, fisherman joined their prey in the shallow water, scooping mounds of fish onto the ice. It was time to sort through the flopping masses of rough fish, mostly carp, suckers, and buffalo, looking for hidden gems. Huge perch, slab crappies, and an occasional northern pike waited to be plucked from the wriggling crowd.

After a few days, one had to climb an ever-growing mound of frozen carcasses just to reach the water. The numbers began to decline. Then they were gone. I never knew if they all died, or if some, with the competition for oxygen diminished, returned to their murky home under the ice.

Surprisingly, the population always seemed to recover. New seed stock swam up from the river or hardy survivors of the holocaust began to reproduce; soon the lake was filled with a new generation of fish, ensuring a continuation of the cycle.

Names and faces disappear through the years, even when the memories of events clearly remain. A boy my age, a relative of our neighbor, Art Kunz, had come for a visit. It was Christmas vacation. The fish had been running so we planned an expedition.

Our equipment was gathered: a silage fork, a burlap bag, and a single pair of hip boots. We shouldered our tools and shortly after noon headed northwest across the snow-covered fields, aiming directly for the lake and the fish. The going was more difficult than we had expected; the calf-high snow made the one and a half mile trip seem much longer. We passed through Mosser's woods and down to the lake; from the shore we could see the mounds of fish on the far side. We had the lake to ourselves.

The numbers were down, but the fishing would have to be classified as good. Turns were taken with the hip boots and the fork, and our pile of fresh fish continued to grow. We grew greedy, adding more and more large crappies and perch to our sack. The cold day grew colder as the sun began to sink in the southwestern sky. It was time to start for home; as it turned out, past time.

It is interesting how a large bag of fish can increase in weight with each step. We left the lake and climbed the low hill into the woods. After a short rest stop and a philosophical discussion, we agreed it would be a good idea to lighten our load. We threw a few of the smallest onto the snow. Our farm came into view a mile away across the snow-covered fields. The sun was going down, and the temperature continued to drop. We were getting tired; we threw out another pile of fish, not bothering to sort them by size. People would still be impressed with our catch.

Despite the loss in weight, the bag continued to plow a deep groove in the soft snow. Wind blew across the open field and evaporated our sweat and chilled our bodies. It became more difficult to lift our feet. We dumped half our fish.

Twice more we lightened our load, the fish and our prestige no longer important. We crossed the road, trudged up the driveway to the house, and dropped a small bag of frozen fish near the back door. We took off our icy boots, slapped the snow from our pants, and hurried into the warm kitchen.

My mother smiled. "Would you boys like a cup of hot chocolate?"

Climbing

A friend told me he had been at my brother Arlo's farm auction in Madelia and had overheard a conversation between two men in the crowd. They were looking across the fields at our home place and were talking about me. One of the men was telling how I used to scramble up and down the outside of our silos like a monkey, seemingly without fear.

He was right except for the fear part. The touch of fear was one of the things that made climbing so attractive.

A short list of my climbing venues, in addition to silos, included trees, barn cupolas, water towers, and to a lesser extent, windmills.

Trees were a specialty and box elders my favorite species. They were large, readily available, and had excellently arranged branches.

I was not a random or purposeless tree climber; my goal was to climb as high as humanly possible, high enough to look out above the tops of the trees. A quick glance at any deciduous tree will quickly reveal the inherent problem: the higher you climb, the smaller the branches become.

I would carefully ascend, selecting the route that followed the thickest limbs. Eventually, as they diminished in size, I would begin swaying, from the wind or from the force of gravity. I was so near. I held several branches together in an attempt to move ever higher, planning at the same time which of those below me I would attempt to grasp if my support collapsed and my direction was suddenly reversed.

The result was always the same. Eventually I would surrender and slowly and carefully retrace my path, sure that the next time I would find the perfect tree and the perfect route to the top.

Depending on their length and size, barns usually have from one to four cupolas. These metal domes, located along the peak of the roof, are designed to vent humid air from the barn. More importantly, they usually housed wild pigeons. Cupolas are not designed for human access.

Access was attained by one of two methods.

Most barns had a large hinged door that folded down against the front of the building. When the haying season was completed, this door was attached to the hay rope and pulled shut with a team of horses or a tractor. The hay rope was then knotted to some structure at the barn's opposite end. The door was now held shut by a taut rope suspended three or four feet below the carrier track that ran the length of the barn.

At the end of the barn opposite the door, about four feet below the peak, was a small platform. This structure was used as a place to stand while performing maintenance on the carrier. The platform was reached by a crude ladder of one-by-four boards nailed between two rows of studs on the end wall.

Pigeons are not welcome in barns; their droppings accumulate beneath their perches and quickly coat and spoil the hay. In spite of the farmer's best efforts, pigeons usually find an entrance, often through broken windowpanes.

I will take you through a typical pigeon-catching event. I quietly sneak into the loft carrying a straw-filled gunnysack. By whatever means available, I stuff the sack into the broken window and chase the trapped birds back and forth until most of them fly into a cupola, normally a safe haven against intruders.

I move to the end of the barn and begin climbing the ladder to the carrier platform. The boards have been in place since shortly after Christ's birth. The wood is rotten and the nails loose and rusty. I test each board, hoping it will support my weight. Each upward step is a small miracle of survival. My head passes above the level of the platform. A pair of nearly-grown baby pigeons startle me, crouched in their flimsy, guano-coated nest. They flare their feathers and peck fiercely, but I ignore their bluff and climb onto the shaky platform.

I grasp the track and step onto the hay rope. The rope sags but soon becomes taut enough to support my weight. Hand over hand, I move along beneath the barn roof, my not-so-tight tightrope swaying beneath my feet. If the barn is filled with hay, I treat my adventure as little more than a lark, but if there is a bare, wooden floor twenty or thirty feet below me, my grip tightens and my knuckles whiten.

I am soon under one of the cupolas. Above, several panicked pigeons are flying wildly around in five-foot circles, their safe haven suddenly becoming a trap. An opening to the cupola straddles one of the barn's rafters. I relinquish the reassuring support of the rope and swing a leg up and over the sharp track. Following a series of gyrations, I am soon sitting upright on the track with my head and torso inserted into the tin structure. I am almost there. I place one hand on the manure-coated barn roof and the other on the centering rafter and pull and push myself erect, all the while attempting to prevent the frantic birds from escaping down past my body.

I have one! I quickly subdue the squirming bird and "lock its wings," a trick little known outside the pigeon catching fraternity. The wings are crossed above the bird's back and then the last joint is crossed again, holding the bird temporarily flightless. If the barn is filled with hay, I drop the captured birds one at a time onto the soft surface, to be retrieved and boxed when I come down. If the barn is empty, the birds are dropped and caught by a sure-handed assistant.

The cupola is now empty, the result of capture or escape, so I retrace my steps, swinging my feet back down to the rope and hand-over-handing it back to the platform. Depending on the pigeon population and my needs and time constraints, I end the hunt or proceed to the next cupola.

Some haymows have doors that open inward instead of folding down in front of the barn. Because it is not needed to hold the doors shut, the rope hangs freely down from the carrier. This suspended rope has two important functions: it can be used as a trapeze to swing back and forth across the barn or it can be climbed to catch pigeons.

When catching pigeons, the rope is used to roll the carrier one way or the other down the track until it is centered under a pigeon-filled cupola. The climber clasps the rope with his hands and legs and crabs his way to the top.

My Uncles Carl and Ed had a huge barn on their "North Farm." It had four cupolas and no hay. My friend Jim Sorenson was my accomplice on my first attempt at scaling the rope and entering these cupolas. I was exhausted by the time I made it to the top of the rope. I clung there, resting my shaky arms and planning my next move. I looked down from the swaying rope at a miniaturized Jim, at the hard floor, and then back up at the cupola, mostly hidden by the carrier. I visualized my next moves: release my leg grip, swing a leg sideways around the carrier and up and over the track, let go of my handhold on the rope and grab the track, and finally, pull my body on top of the track and into the cupola. I slid back down the rope.

Jim took his turn on the rope and successfully navigated all the difficulties. He dropped a couple of pigeons down that I deftly caught and placed in a gunny sack.

Challenged and more determined, I took my turn at the next cupola, this time navigating the obstacles and capturing my share of the prey. I remember feeling a little dizzy as I looked down from the bowels of the cupola to the hard surface below. I maneuvered beneath the track and back onto the rope. I know it was a relief to slide down the rope and get my feet back on the floor. A few minutes later it was my turn to tackle another cupola.

Some may wonder, "Why did you want the pigeons; what good were they?" I can't really say. Perhaps, like climbing mountains, it was "because they were there." I sometimes put them in an old shed and kept them as wild pets until they eventually escaped, and I once cleaned several and had my mom cook them. As to how they tasted, please refer to the "once." Sometimes I harkened to the farmer's code pertaining to any nuisance species and killed them.

Our silos were fifty feet tall and made from interlocking cement staves held in place by steel hoops that wrapped around the structure about three feet apart. A row of square doors extended up the front and was enclosed by a semicircular metal chute. Beginning in late fall, farmers would climb up the inside of the chute each day and throw silage down into a waiting wagon or onto a pile that was later carried off to feed the cows. The chute made the climb from door to door seem relatively safe.

It was also possible to climb outside the safety of the chute, an activity I considered recreational climbing. A three-inch gap between the steel rods and the silo allowed enough space to grab on with your hands and to stand on with the balls of your feet. Climbing was regulated by height. Much as some carnivals have signs reading, "You must be this tall to go on this ride," you had to be a certain height to climb our silos. A climber's reach, from their upstretched hands to tips of their toes, had to span three hoops.

You would reach high and grasp the hoop above you, take one giant step to the hoop near your waist, pull yourself up straight, and reach up and grab the next higher hoop. From this point on, as FDR once said, you had nothing to fear but fear itself.

"Let's go climb the silo" was a cry often heard at our farm, one that was usually uttered by me. I guess I liked showing off to those who were less brave or less foolish than I was. They would usually make it ten or twenty feet before freezing and carefully returning to the ground, squeezing each rod in a death grip as they descended. I, in the meantime, would climb to the top and back or up and down in the general vicinity of the beginner, offering sage advice and encouragement.

Silo climbing was usually a solitary activity; I spent hours playing on the silo. I remember tying hay bale twine strings together to form a long rope and fastening one end of the rope to my belt and the other end to a sand-filled pail. I climbed to the top and straddled the upper edge, one leg in and one leg out, then pulled the pail up and emptied the sand into the silo. I lowered the pail and climbed down and refilled it, repeating the process until the silo was full or until I became bored.

Climbing didn't seem too dangerous during the ascent because you were staring at a safe looking, monochromatic cement foreground. It was when your eyes cleared the top of the silo and you looked down into the deep cavern in front of you or glanced down at the distant ground, that you sometimes questioned the wisdom of your recent decision.

Climbing up and down was time consuming. There wasn't much I could do to increase the speed of the upward climb; you can't run up a silo. The descent, on the other hand, could be greatly accelerated. I developed a technique best described as a modified free fall. With my toes against the silo, I would drop downward, releasing my hand and foot holds at the same time. As I dropped from one pair of hoops to the next, my hands and feet would make brief contact with the rods, just enough to slow my fall and keep me close to the silo.

There aren't many things I regret or would change about my childhood. If I were forced to make a list, this method of descending our silo would be near the top. I still get a queasy feeling in the pit of my stomach when I think how dangerous it was. One slip or miscalculation was all it would have taken.

Mom's flower garden in front of one of our tall silos. The shorter silo is what remains of another that was broken off during the tornado that flattened much of our farm the year before I was born.

Dogs

I was born into a two-dog family. Pal, a small brown and white rat terrier, lived in the house and Big Pup, also brown and white, probably a cross between a collie and some kind of shepherd, claimed the barn as his residence. I suppose I was on a first name basis with both but not really old enough to interact or bond with either.

I must begin with an account of the heeking incident. Pal was my sister Marlys' dog. The two of them would huddle for hours beside the woodbox behind our old cook stove. Mar would gently and repeatedly grasp the fur behind Pal's ears and slowly slide the hairs between her thumb and forefinger, an activity she referred to as heeking. Looking back, it appears as if heeking was a mutual obsession.

All the Feder families made an annual Christmas Eve pilgrimage to Grandma Lena's house in Madelia. On this particular evening we were paid a surprise visit by Santa Claus. Santa wandered around the room picking up each child in turn, eager to discuss their Christmas wants and the status of their past year's behavior. He leaned down and picked up Marlys, going directly to his greatest concern: "I'm sure you have been a good girl. You haven't been heeking your dog again, have you?" Mar looked Santa directly in the eye with a combination of guilt and stubborn determination written across her face. "No," she lied.

We came down to breakfast one morning to discover that terrible tragedy had struck during the night. Pal was missing; he had run away. The sadness lingered for many days but gradually faded. I'm not sure how old you are when you can first see out of a kitchen window while standing on a chair. Several weeks after the big disappearance, Mother was working at the table, preparing dinner for guests, and I was standing on the chair, peering over the windowsill. There on the ground, looking up, was Pal.

"Pal's home," I cried. Mom hurried to the window, and her disbelief changed to a different look, one I didn't recognize. Pal wagged up at us.

Our happiness was short-lived. A few days later Pal "ran away" again.

Secrets leak out. By the time I reached adulthood, I had pieced together small clues relating to Pal's disappearance. Pal had begun to snap at strangers. Pal had been "dropped off" somewhere near Hanska, a dozen miles to the northwest. Complete details remain sketchy, but the Pal problem was eventually put to rest, if you get my meaning.

Me, Marlys, and Pal, when I was one year old.

Big Pup was my father's dog. I imagine his name had evolved with his size and age. Little kids didn't cling to or cuddle with Big Pup; he was a dog's dog, preferring to hang out in the barn or follow Dad around the farm.

Big Pup had one glaring and mighty weakness: he was terrified of thunder and lightning. Dad tried locking him in the barn in an attempt to shield him from his fears. For as long as I lived on the farm, the jagged, tooth-gnawed, dog-sized escape hole in the corner of our inch-and-a-half-thick barn door reminded me of the plan's failure.

One morning after a serious nighttime storm, we came down to breakfast to find Big Pup cowering in a corner of our house's entryway. A big hole had been gnawed through the wooden storm door. The door was replaced, and as long as we had Big Pup, a row of porcelain electric fence insulators and their accompanying wires waited to be connected to a charger at the first sign of a storm building in the west.

Pal and Big Pup were gone by the time I was four years old. After several dog-less years, Vickie arrived on our farm. Vickie was a beautiful female collie and the best dog ever. She was smart, friendly, and playful. She technically belonged to all of us, but she and my brother Arlo were inseparable. When she was two years old, Vickie developed cancer and died. I remember crying on my mother's lap, aching all over from my loss.

"We'll get another dog."

"I don't want another dog," I sobbed. "I want Vickie."

We did get another dog. I came home from school one day to find a new female collie named Robin wandering our farm. Robin had big paws to fill and turned out to be startlingly deficient in doing so. She was wild and sneaky and showed absolutely no interest in any of us. I now realize she hadn't been properly socialized as a puppy and should be forgiven her behavior, but at the time she just seemed mean and unfriendly. Robin's stay lasted two weeks. The return to her original owner was hastened when we caught her with a dead chicken and a mouth full of feathers, both unpardonable sins on any farm.

Border collies and English shepherds are both respectable, hardworking breeds. Blackie, a cross between the two, turned out to be the black dog of the family. Dad tried to teach him to guard the cattle gate so our steers wouldn't escape when the feed wagon was driven into the lot, a task any responsible herding dog should relish. Blackie would have none of that foolishness; he wanted to play, not work. Looking back, I can see a lot of similarities between the two of us.

Blackie liked to follow tractors in the field. Branching out, he learned to follow our pickup when we drove on our old dirt road to work at our "Other Farm," the farm where my brother Arlo and his wife Mary now live. Sometimes when the dirt road had turned to mud and was impassable, we would take the long way around on the gravel roads. Blackie would watch us get into the pickup. If we turned south to use the gravel route, he would take off across the fields at a dead run; when we reached the farm he would be waiting with his tongue hanging out and his tail wagging. We often turned the same direction when we went to town but on those occasions Blackie would just watch us go.

We never learned how he could tell which times we were going to the Other Farm and which times we were going to town.

We were treated to an interesting display of animal behavior during Blackie's reign. Our beautiful riding horse, Tony, got loose one day and became tangled in barbed wire. Dad, who grew up driving and training horses, was amazed at Tony's response. Instead of panicking and thrashing to pull free as horses usually did, even though he was badly cut on his back legs, Tony calmly waited until Dad found and freed him. One of the cuts, just above a back hoof, was exceptionally deep. Dad was worried that in spite of medical treatment, infection would set in and was sure if Tony recovered he would be lame.

Tony was tied in one of our horse stalls, and Blackie immediately began his own special treatment. Many times a day he would stop by and carefully lick the wounds on Tony's legs. Amazingly, not only did infection not set in, but the cuts healed so fast that in a few weeks we were riding and running Tony as if nothing had happened.

Dad, me, and Arlo riding a fully recovered Tony.

From time to time, Blackie turned up missing and rumors began to reach us that a dog that looked a lot like him was being seen in various parts of our neighborhood. One day my mother came out of a grocery store on Main Street and there, down the sidewalk, was Blackie, hanging out with a group of his buddies. Blackie saw Mother at the same time and trotted over to say hello with his head cocked to one side and his tail wagging. He had a friendly smile on his face and was sure she was as happy to see him as he was to see her.

The code for farm dogs is a strict one. No good can come from dogs that wander and run in packs. Sheep and deer can be killed and liability and the fear of criticism by neighbors become real concerns. Blackie was forced to pay the most severe penalty for his newly-acquired lifestyle.

Buster moved to our farm when I was a sophomore in high school and grew to become a big gentle collie. No drama or excitement here; Buster was friendly, calm, and possibly a little boring. Like his immediate predecessors, he did no guarding, herding, or work of any kind, but on the other hand, he didn't wander, chase cats, kill chickens, or bark like a fool. He fulfilled our modest expectations of what a farm dog should be.

Near the end of Buster's tour of duty, I left the farm to attend college, leaving Arlo in charge of our canine situation. He performed admirably and continued our long line of Feder dogs.

Arlo and Vickie

THE PHILSOPHER

Carl carried a spoon in the breast pocket of his bib overalls. He was a small man and on all occasions wore the overalls, a blue work shirt, and a grizzled, week-grown beard.

With or without prompting, Carl was more than willing to expound on the three things that made life worthwhile: drinking beer, eating ice cream, and, in more crudely worded language, making love to women.

I was witness to one of Carl's passions. Saturday evenings he would come into Adolf's store, remove a pint of vanilla from the freezer, fish out his spoon, find a stool in the back corner, and methodically empty the container.

One of a group of young boys, anxious to understand the intricacies of life, approached with a question: "Carl, which of your interests do you like best?"

Carl rubbed his gray stubble for a moment.

"Whichever one I'm doing."

THE CRUSH

Our neighbor, Kay Murphy, had recently returned home. Divorced. One summer day she called and asked if I would stop at her parent's farm. Her two stepchildren were visiting from Texas. Sonny was ten and Betty twelve, a year younger than me. They were both quiet and fun, fascinating with their soft southern drawls. We played together two or three times before they returned home.

The following summer, I was at Buster Yates' rodeo grounds, helping some recently acquired cowboy friends prepare for the weekend's performance. I looked up. There, through the arena fence was Betty, watching me with a shy smile.

The next week I rode my horse, Tony, to the Murphy farm. Sonny, Betty, and I spent much of the afternoon running, playing games, and being kids.

Later, we hid from Sonny in a small clump of bushes near the road and talked for a long time. I had thought, like me, everyone had grown up in a safe and protecting home. She was beautiful with brown hair and soft blue eyes. I almost kissed her.

The afternoon was nearly gone. I leaned over Tony's neck and galloped out the driveway and up the road. Showing off.

I think of her sometimes.

Field And Stream

A beautiful trout arches above a whitewater stream, its multicolored side gleaming in the sunlight. A vibrating line leading to a fly in the corner of its mouth sprays beads of water into the morning air.

The cover of the June 1953 *Field and Stream* magazine is as clear in my mind as the day I brought it home nearly sixty years ago. It was not the cover that changed my life, but the content. A world of hunting, fishing, and outdoor adventure opened before my eyes, a world where grown men were bonded together by a time-honored code of camaraderie and sportsmanship.

Southern gentlemen carefully protected their quail coveys. They planted food plots and wildlife cover in the corners of their fields and along fencerows. Self-imposed limits insured the birds' survival for this and many years to follow.

Hunters awoke in the early morning darkness. They fought through splashing waves to reed-covered blinds, their faces stung by sharp needles of snow and sleet. Wings whistled overhead. The men hunkered down and waited for first light and the flocks of bluebills that would set their wings and bank into the decoys.

Fishermen matched wits with great lunkers hidden beneath sunken snags, mats of water lilies, or among the rocks of fast-moving streams. The array of ammunition was seemingly unlimited. Hula Poppers, Dardevles, and Jitterbugs were cast on lakes and ponds, and flies with exotic names like Royal Coachman, Muddlers, and March Browns were floated across sheltered pools or dragged through raging whitewater rapids.

The dogs! There were coonhounds, foxhounds, and wolfhounds. There were pointers and setters for hunting upland birds and feist dogs and beagles for chasing squirrels and rabbits. No self-respecting waterfowl hunter would brave the lakes and marshes without his trusty black lab or golden retriever.

If all this wasn't exciting enough, the back pages were filled with marvelous advertisements. Who could possibly survive without knowing how to raise New Zealand White rabbits for fun and profit or how to restore your wetland and attract ducks by planting sago pondweed or wild celery? I remember taking fifty cents from my carefully guarded hoard and buying fifty penny postcards. For the next few weeks, and even the next few years, our mailbox was flooded with wonderful opportunities for the budding outdoorsman.

The autumns of my youth were decided. Most mornings I would turn off my alarm, eat a big bowl of cereal, put on my hip boots, and head out the door. Our sloughs provided duck hunting from early October until mid-November and mink and muskrat trapping from then until the end of the year. I made duck decoys and rafts. I walked the cornfields and marshes for pheasants and rode my bike to fish for bullheads in Fedge Lake.

I subscribed to *Field and Stream*, *Sports Afield*, and *Outdoor Life*. I knew I would never attain the lofty designation of sportsman, but in my mind I was in league with men who had.

A survivor from the set of decoys I made when I was a kid.

CATTLE

Our life revolved around cattle. All the corn grown on our farm eventually climbed bellowing up the loading chute, into the big semis, and down the highway to the South St. Paul Stockyards.

Mom gently shook my shoulder; it was four o'clock. I pulled on my clothes and, half awake, stumbled down to the kitchen. I finished a big bowl of Grape-Nuts and helped Dad carry the suitcases out the back door into the cool fall air. I was skipping school and we were on our way to South Dakota; things couldn't get much better than that.

It was early in the week; we had to be in Huron by mid-morning. I lasted a few miles, then climbed in back, pulled a blanket off the seat, and curled up on the floor. No place in the world was better for sleeping, even if I had to choose between draping myself over the big center hump or curling up off to one side. I listened to the soothing hum of the tires and in no time was sound asleep.

"Where are we?" I poked my head above the seat, blinking in the bright sunlight. We were in South Dakota with only an hour to go. Dad drove us into a station for gas and a quick second breakfast before continuing on to Huron.

We walked down the manure-splashed alleys and carefully inspected the cattle. Climbing a couple of boards up, we could see over the tops of the tall wooden fences. If a pen looked promising, we opened the gate and walked among the milling animals. Some groups were tame, cattle that had been around people; others, recently rounded up from the open range, were white-eyed and frightened. Long, dangerous horns clicked and rattled as a herd of three-year-olds parted, fighting to keep their distance.

If the price was too good to pass up, Dad might consider bringing home big cattle like these, but the initial investment was usually too great to gamble on. It was mostly this year's calves, those weighing around five hundred pounds, that we had come to see. The calves were having a hard time; recently weaned from their mothers, they were hungry, lonesome, and frightened. The bellowing in the calf pens was high-pitched, rasping, and continuous.

The Huron barn was at a disadvantage. Dad was not yet sure what should be considered bargain prices for the week, so we moved on empty-handed. The days went by: Fort Pierre, Phillip, Sturgis, and Belle Fourche.

Dad might sit quietly for two or three days, then suddenly the ring man was looking directly at him. Dad was bidding. The price began creeping upward, driven by his almost imperceptible nod, first by a penny a pound, then half cents and finally fourths. The ring man pleaded and begged; somewhere in the crowd another buyer was getting the same treatment. The gavel fell. We were the owners of forty Hereford steer calves weighing five hundred and twenty-three pounds.

The auction ended but much more work remained to be done. A long line crept slowly through the smoky sale barn office. Each buyer in turn tore a check from his book, filled it out – in some cases for an unbelievably large sum – and pocketed his receipt. The receipt would be needed later to gain the release of the newly purchased livestock. We next stood in line at a long bank of phones that stretched along one wall. Sometimes we arranged local trucking but usually we called Big Pete back in Madelia. In a few hours he would have one or more of his big Kenworths on the road. Finally, we made a call to my mother, letting her know when the trucks would be arriving; more often than not it would be in the middle of the night.

When we had purchased enough steers to fill our feedlot, we headed home, hoping to get there before these last cattle arrived. Two or three big rigs would crowd into our yard or line up along the road. The drivers, sitting high in their cabs, would stare into their mirrors, and crank the big steering wheels, and magically the long trailers would back through the narrow cattle yard gate. A long ramp was pulled out from under the floor of the semi and big wooden gates were unhooked from the sides of the truck and attached to the ramp. The rear door was rolled up and the cattle began pouring down the shaky temporary chute. The frightened steers took a lap or two around the feedlot before they slowly calmed down and began to investigate their new home.

Now began a most critical period, one that could determine an entire year's profit or loss. The herd would be fine for a few days, learning to drink from the tank and eating the fresh hay we kept in the mangers. Then the coughing would begin. Shipping fever. This disease, actually pneumonia, was brought on by the stresses of weaning, exhaustion, and the cold drafts in the trucks. We watched the calves carefully; those not eating were immediately separated, driven into a head gate, and administered shots of penicillin. Most of the calves improved in two or three days, began eating again, and were turned back with the herd. Despite our best efforts, some died. A loss of two or three was acceptable, more was disappointing, and a loss of many was disastrous.

Dead animals were hooked to a chain and pulled from the barn or cattle pens into an open space in our yard; a day or two later the rendering truck would arrive. The loading process was disgusting but too fascinating not to watch. The truck was backed up to the bloated animal and its big rusty metal rear door swung wide. A flood of stench poured from the box, engulfing everyone and everything in its wake.

A lever was engaged and a heavy steel cable began unwinding from a steel drum at the front of the truck box. The driver grabbed the free end of the cable and pulled it toward the carcass. The end was looped around the neck of the deceased and the lever reversed. The cable began rewinding on the drum, slowly dragging the animal forward toward the truck, then upward, and finally over a rounded end at the back of the truck's box. Throughout the entire process the animal's neck continued to stretch until it seemed impossible not to separate from the body.

At the front of the truck were the fruits of the driver's earlier stops: a dead horse, a big Holstein, and two or three pigs. Gasses and fluids oozed from the menagerie as our steer was dragged to the top. The driver climbed into the truck, unhooked the chain, and returned to the cab. He removed his greasy leather gloves, handed my dad a few pencils or a calendar, and headed for his next stop.

Some years the calves were dehorned when we purchased them; buyers were willing to pay a premium if this dangerous and costly chore was completed in advance of the sale. Many times, however, this chore fell on us. Dr. Bohen would arrive with his specially designed dehorning chute and the calves were driven in one at a time, their heads strapped solidly in place. Doc would grab his saw, remove each horn with a few quick strokes, extract the primary artery with a special forceps, and cove the wound with a white clotting powder. The door was swung open.

Next!

The bellowing calf would run wildly back to the herd. Soon animals were standing in small clusters or isolated in remote corners, dazed, blood dripping from their lowered heads. This was one of the days I preferred to be in school.

Dad had a beautiful team of matched Belgiums, sorrels with light manes and tails. Twice daily they were harnessed, led from the barn, and hitched to the feed wagon. Up and down the rows of bunks they went, Dad forking or shoveling the feed and the horses moving or stopping at his quiet command. Sometimes when the chores were finished, Dad would unhook the team and lift me high on one of their wide backs. The horses would trot into the barn and crowd into their stall, eager for their oats and hay. I was forced to duck as my horse passed through the barn door to avoid being scraped off.

Our cemented feedlot was well protected from winter winds, guarded on the north by the big barn and on the west by a tall, eight-foot cement stave fence. A twelve-inch diameter post was set into the ground at the north end of the fence. This was probably the most important place on our farm, for it was over this post that a loop of chain was dropped, keeping the big wooden cattle yard gate locked.

Next to fire or tornados, our greatest fear was of hearing the alarm "The cattle are out!"

The post was sufficiently tall to prevent a boy from opening it until at least some sense of responsibility had been drilled into his head. "Did you lock the gate?" was an often-heard expression.

The gate was level; if it was open, it would stay open and if it was shut, it would remain shut. Unfortunately, if the chain was not put in place, a west wind could blow and hold it open. I remember the guilt I felt if, after working in the lot, I came out and found I had not secured the gate. Sometimes Dad would get dressed in the night and go out to check the gate, some little voice warning him he may not have closed it properly.

Most mishaps were minor and temporary, usually taking place at chore time. Someone would pull a wagon or drive a tractor into the lot and before they could park and get back to the gate, a few steers would escape, usually wandering around just outside the fence. It certainly helped to have assistance in getting them back because when the gate was left open to chase them in, more would come out and join the escapees. A "Hey, Rube!" call would go out for anyone in the house or yard to come and assist with the roundup.

We awoke one morning to find cattle everywhere. They were going in and out of the gate and up and down the driveway. Streams of steers were walking down the road or into our fields. Some stood on the backside of the yard, staring in through the board fence.

You could see the stress on Dad's face. He had one firm command: "Don't chase them." He drove to the neighbors to let them know the cattle were out and to give them the same message. Steers that in the feedlot were tame and gentle could turn white-eyed with panic in a strange environment. Running could turn into stampeding as they fed off each other's fear.

The plan was straightforward: all remaining cattle were locked in the barn or the back lot, and the big cattle yard gate was tied open. We would wait. Gradually, small clumps of steers began wandering back into the yard and through the gate. Each returning group was added to those safely secured in the barn. I think it was the third day before the last of the vagabond cattle finally straggled into our yard. Their return was primarily motivated by thirst; luckily they had found no open water within the scope of their travels.

Dad was the only one who knew how many steers we owned. I'm sure he kept an accurate count of the returnees and of the number still at large. In the end, the only financial loss was from the weight lost due to stress and hunger. A few days later the cattle were relaxed and back on feed. The danger and fear of liability claims were lost to young boys, but I'm sure not to the adults in the family.

I never heard or knew if blame was assigned. I was just happy that for once I wasn't the one responsible.

Several times each year the big barn was cleaned. The SC Case with its mounted manure loader snaked around the supporting posts, hauling the semi-solid manure outside of the barn. In summers or open winters, the manure was deposited in a waiting spreader and hauled directly to the fields, but in snowy winters it was dumped on a great pile in the cattle yard and spread the following spring. The job of cleaning the barn was a good half-day's work. I remember as a small boy, before we owned a tractor and loader, watching my father and the hired men toil for days as they cleaned the barn by hand using five-tined manure forks.

The fun part came after the barn was clean. Bales of oat straw were carried in and broken open in rows down the length of the barn. The steers followed, playing and fighting with each newly opened bale. They bawled and grunted and shoved as they tossed the straw with their heads and hooves. The straw was soon spread evenly throughout the barn and the steers were standing in the fresh, dry bedding, quietly chewing their cuds.

Herb, me, and Vic, our Hubbard Milling Company feed representative. It was difficult maintaining my balance on the frozen clumps of manure.

The work of caring for cattle was compounded in winter; water and water lines froze, engines refused to start, silage stuck to the sides of the silo, and moving parts became immobile and then broke. Snow accumulated and vehicles became stuck or buried.

Blizzards struck.

The wind switched to the northeast and the air grew damp and heavy. Big fluffy flakes began drifting down. The afternoon chores went on as usual, but a kind of anticipation or forewarning seemed to fill the air.

Darkness came earlier than normal. The winds gradually increased and the flakes grew smaller and began blowing horizontally. We listened to Cedric Adams' ten o'clock news, and I took one last look at the yard light; visibility was definitely diminishing. I climbed the stairs and wrapped myself in my covers, secure in the knowledge that school would be closed tomorrow.

I awoke at first light and pressed my nose against my window. The wind was howling and had switched to the northwest during the night. Gusts pounded against the siding and rattled the panes. I searched through my drawer and dug out a set of thermal underwear, the arms and legs too short as usual. Mom and Dad were eating breakfast and the radio was tuned to the *World News Roundup*. No need to listen to the local weather; we only had to look outside.

Dad went out ahead of me, started the Case with the snow bucket, and began tackling the biggest drifts. There was no point in doing a good job; the snow would soon fill in again. By the time I found my warmest clothes and put on my five-buckle overshoes, he had the wagon parked against the silo. The team stood patiently as huge forkfuls of silage rattled down the chute to the wagon below.

I opened and closed the big board gate. As Dad drove the team to the first bunk, the cattle left the security of the barn and closed in behind the wagon, hungry, fighting for position. The snow melted when it first struck their warm bodies but soon began to accumulate. Backs, and then faces and eyelashes, were soon coated in white. No lollygagging today; as soon as the feed was gone, the animals crowded back into the barn.

A large barn packed with steers is a unique place. The air is warm and humid as puffs of vapor rise with each breath the animals take. My nostrils fill with a not-unpleasant blend of manure, methane, wet hair, and hay. I climb the steps to the haymow and am shocked by the instant temperature change from warm to ice cold. I begin breaking open bales of alfalfa and throwing the hay down the holes to the mangers below. Above each hole, the rising humid air has coated the walls and surrounding hay with a frosty hoar.

The storm rages on. We finish the morning chores, shake off the excess snow and tromp into the basement to hang up our wet clothes. Now comes a strange but somehow happy time. For one of the few times all year, Dad relaxes and rests during a workday. The remainder of the morning and early afternoon are spent in the living room, with Dad napping on the couch or reading the paper while Mom and the rest of us read books, put together puzzles, or play games.

The storm has let up by the time afternoon chore time arrives, but the temperatures are falling and the snow is still blowing and drifting. My enthusiasm for storms is definitely waning.

The seasons progress through spring, summer, and into early fall. The steers are healthy and have been growing on their diet of ground corn and soybean meal. Dad is changing as well. Each day at exactly 12:35 p.m., all conversation at the dinner table stops as Dad gives us a stern look and turns up the volume on the radio. "And now here is Lyle Lamphere with a look at today's market." For five minutes, Lyle discusses and analyzes the morning's sales from the South St. Paul market. Each dollar or two change per hundredweight will have an important impact on our year's income.

Dad continues to closely monitor both the cattle and the market. One day he decides it's time to ship. The steers are driven through a narrow passage and each animal deemed ready is placed in a separate pen. I could never understand my father's exact criteria, but eventually we would have one or two truckloads of the largest and fattest steers enclosed in the pen between our two barns.

Big Pete is once again called. The big semis are loaded late in the day to prevent as much weight loss as possible before the next morning's sale. The trailer shakes and rattles as it fills with twelve-hundred-pound steers. A last word with Dad and the drivers climb aboard. They roll the big trucks down the driveway, and the banks of amber lights disappear into the darkness.

Marketing cattle was a complex business. The South St. Paul market was one of the biggest in the country, their yards a maze of pens and alleys. Farmers would select a brokerage company to sell his cattle for him. We always consigned to the largest, Central Livestock Association.

The truckers unloaded at the north end of the stockyards and yard employees drove the cattle to the pens of the selected agent. Early the next morning, buyers from the big packing companies, Swift and Armor, moved through the pens to purchase livestock for the day's kill. A representative, in our case from Central, would haggle with the buyers, attempting to obtain the best possible price for his customer.

Dad wanted to be in the yards when the buyers arrived. He and his brothers were considered big feeders, and Dad always felt his presence motivated the Central agents to bargain for that little extra half or quarter cent a pound that added to our profit. I was often allowed to tag along, again getting up early in the morning. The yards were an exciting place. Gates were swung, warnings shouted, and cattle seemed to be everywhere. It was our responsibility to scramble up the fences to avoid getting trampled and from receiving dirty looks from the yardmen. Pens were filled with cattle of every color, steers with gigantic horns and bulls fighting and mounting each other. By mid-morning the sale was completed, the check in my dad's pocket, and we were on our way home, still time to get in a good half-day's work.

Below is a photo of the two of us standing in the yards the morning our steers topped the market. I believe they sold for thirty-eight and a half cents a pound, the all-time Stockyard record. A week or two later we were looking at the comics section of the Minneapolis Tribune and, in one corner of a small section reserved for humorous anecdotes, was the verse: "Ervin Feder is the feeder of top feeder cattle."

The days we didn't have time to go to the yards we listened on the radio to find out how our cattle had done. After his general analysis of the day's market, Lyle would announce: "Now let's move down to each of the alleys for the details of today's trade." Each "alley" referred to hogs, sheep, and cattle; we were only interested in the latter.

Dad would put his ear close to the radio and signal for quiet as Mr. Lamphere went down the list. Finally: "Peterson Trucking of Madelia hauling forty-seven whiteface steers bringing thirty-two cents, weighing twelve hundred thirty-three pounds." I would ask if we had received a good price but usually received a rather noncommittal answer. Dad would get up, walk into the living room, lie down on the couch for his usual twenty-minute noon nap, and then go back outside to work.

Over the next few weeks our lot continued to empty until, at last, only the "small end" remained. These too eventually fattened to Dad's standard and were shipped. Our feedlot was empty.

The corn was picked and the fall plowing nearly completed. Dad closely watched the feeder market, planning his trip to South Dakota.

Magical Morning

This event took place when I was about thirteen, not old enough to have a driver's license, but easily old enough to drive on the isolated country roads around our farm. An interesting thing is that the importance, wonder, and clarity of this day has continued to grow in my mind instead of fading like so many early memories.

A fox had dug a fresh den near the west end of the eighty-acre field on what we knew as the "Other Farm." This is the field north of where my brother Arlo and his wife Mary now live. The far end of the field was slightly sandy, "light soil" my dad called it. The fox had taken advantage of the soil conditions and had dug its hole deep into the slope of a slight rise.

I had recently armed myself with a new Marlin 22 rifle and had acquired new hunting skills, thanks to *Field and Stream* magazine. Having learned that fox were exceptionally wily and wise, I decided the best way to shoot one would be to outsmart it.

Fox are nocturnal; if I positioned myself in the perfect place I could ambush it at sunrise, when it returned to its den. The assigned morning, in late April or early May, came early. I got up in the dark, probably about four, ate a quick bowl of Grape-Nuts, and drove along our old field road. I parked in the field driveway, carefully checked the wind direction so as to approach from the downwind side and, as quietly as possible, walked the half-mile length of the field. About thirty yards south of the den I lowered myself into my best military prone position and waited.

I stared into the nearly-black darkness and hoped the fox didn't return before I could see well enough to get off an accurate shot. A rosy glow began to fill the eastern sky. Conditions were perfect. All my senses sharpened as I waited in anticipation; still no fox. Gradually the morning brightened and the sun appeared over the horizon. What didn't appear was the fox. My patience exhausted and my body stiff, I accepted defeat, stood up, and looked around. What I saw is as clear to me as if it happened yesterday.

Across the fencerow at the northwest corner of the field, in our neighbor's brushy, mostly unused pasture, was an immense thicket of wild plum trees. The white blossoms seemed to glow in the early morning sunlight, and a light northerly breeze gently covered me with the sweet scent of the flowers. The blossoms and the perfume were not what I thought about or what I looked at. The trees were filled with small birds.

They flitted. They chased each other and bounced from tree to tree. They were red, yellow, black and white, or multicolored. The air was filled with their calls and songs. I will never forget that moment, standing with the warm morning sun at my back and the trees alive with small birds. Understanding was not necessary.

Years later I went to college, took a class in ornithology, bought a pair of binoculars, and became a birder. I know now I was watching warblers newly arrived from Central and South America. I was experiencing what is known as a wave. The birds fly across the Gulf of Mexico and begin gradually working their way north with the warming weather. If they hit an area of cold or snow, they stop their northerly trek and are joined day after day by more warblers. When the inclement weather breaks, the birds continue their journey toward the northern forests, now clumped together in a super flock of migrants.

Sometimes the congregation stops to feed and rest in the morning sun and fill a young boy with wonder.

ICE SLEDDING

The stars were obviously aligned; it was one of those rare early winters when the ice had frozen on a clear, calm night, forming an absolutely glass-smooth sheet. Snow had stayed away and cold temperatures had frozen the ice several inches thick. My Cousin David arrived at our farm with his latest invention.

He had somehow attached makeshift chains around the tires of his Harley and had just taken it for a spin on Wilson's Lake. The maiden voyage had been a success. Did I think it would be fun to be pulled around the lake on a sled? I hope by this time you know my answer. I found a long rope in the machine shed, grabbed up my Flexible Flyer, our old metal runner sled, and climbed on behind David. We took the road to Mosser's and then down through the pasture to the lake.

Dave accelerated across the ice with me trailing thirty or forty feet behind. Having your face a few inches from a sheet of ice can greatly magnify the sense of speed, especially when you are traveling fifty miles an hour. He eased her to a stop so we could discuss our next move.

We built up as much speed as Dave thought he could handle. He started his turn to the left and my sled began to slide, centrifugal force accelerating me around the turn. Dave sharpened his turn. Soon the runners on my sled were emitting a shearing scream as I slid absolutely sideways across the ice. I now know that even a seemingly perfect sheet of ice has minor flaws and tiny imperfections. The sled launched and rolled. Where it ended up was of no importance to me; I was no longer aboard.

Friction will eventually stop a sliding, rolling object. I climbed to my feet as David swung the rig around and pulled to a stop. "Let's go again."

Ice sledding is a little known and mostly forgotten sport, but for one day, it was king.

Impeach Earl Warren

My dad and uncles fed cattle. Each fall they traveled to the major sale barns in South Dakota to replenish their recently emptied feedlots. I was often allowed to tag along. The trips provided travel, adventure, and most importantly, days off from school.

Despite a banner above the highway at Lake Benton declaring "Where the West Begins," Minnesota did not end at the border. It straggled on, its corn and bean fields surviving in fits and starts until, finally, at the Missouri River, the transformation was complete and Minnesota gave way to the hills and grasslands of South Dakota. Cattle country.

The change in landscape was not the only transformation. Roadside signs that had, until now, foretold the distance between towns or the location of rest stops, suddenly created an advertising hell.

I never knew anyone who used Burma-Shave but the signs were ubiquitous. "Does your husband / Misbehave / Grunt and grumble / Rant and rave / Shoot the brute some / Burma-Shave." The variations were endless.

It was impossible to get lost; you always knew how far you were from Wall Drug. There were signs for every kind of roadside attraction: cement dinosaurs, palaces covered with corn, reptile gardens, grotesque land formations, prairie dog towns, ghost towns, jackalopes, and faces carved in mountains. Signs for petrified wood, five cent coffee, and snakeskin cowboy boots.

It was your last chance for gas, free ice water, the Badlands, or Wild Bill Hickok.

I was fourteen when a new kind of sign appeared; they were everywhere. Painted on barns, plastered on billboards, nailed to posts, or hung from fences. They were professionally designed or smeared by amateurs using old paintbrushes. "Impeach Earl Warren."

I had no idea what was happening. Who exactly was Earl Warren and what had he done to deserve impeachment? What exactly was impeachment? It sounded painful.

A question here, a history class there; eventually I began to figure some of it out. Earl was Chief Justice of the United States Supreme Court, not in itself an actual crime. He had presided over a case, Brown vs. the Board of Education, that had desegregated schools in the South. Hardly a South Dakota problem to my way of thinking. The state had maybe eleven black people. There was something deeper.

Prejudice was hard for a fourteen-year-old boy to understand. It still is for some grownups.

A Lesson In Speed

Our neighbor, Art Kunz, brought his baler and wagon to our farm to bale a few loads of straw for my dad. In addition to his rig, he brought along a worker to stack bales on the rack, Shorty Lawrence. Shorty may have been short in some worlds, but he towered above me.

School was only a few weeks away. Shorty was among a group of students from St. Mary's Catholic School who would be transferring to our freshman class. I didn't know Shorty well but, in the banter that developed between us, the topic arose as to which of us was the faster runner. Knowing full well I was faster, I challenged him to a game of tag. I took off across the stubble field with Shorty in pursuit; he was surprisingly fast, but by cutting and turning I avoided being touched. Those who knew Shorty will understand when I say that, even at that age, he was not a well-conditioned athlete. Pulling up panting he remarked, "Wait until I'm not wearing work boots and we run in a straight line." I saw these comments for what they were: an obvious attempt to save face.

One afternoon in late spring of my freshman year, Mr. Paulson, our principal and track coach, came to gym class with an announcement: the Middle Eight Conference Track and Field Meet would be held the following Friday. The meet would include a freshman relay and he wanted to find the four fastest runners in our class. I had no doubt I would be included in that group.

The entire class was lined up across the street in preparation for the one-block race. At the signal "Go," I took off at a sprint. Something was wrong. Classmates I had always been able to outrun slowly pulled ahead of me. I strained my utmost before gradually slowing at the finish line in crushed resignation.

Shorty Lawrence finished first and I placed a poor sixth. I was bewildered and disappointed. I suppose what I needed most at the time, but never received, was a lesson in human growth and development. Or perhaps Shorty had just given me one.

SWANS

I was a freshman the snowy, late-March afternoon I came home from school to find a flock of swans swimming in our south slough. I had never seen wild swans. Quickly I changed into my everyday winter clothes, strapped my hip boots to my belt, and crossed the fence into Lindstrom's pasture.

Snowflakes the size of quarters filled the sky, limiting visibility and muffling sound. I walked across the short-grazed pasture; neither the water nor the swans were visible until I reached the reeds and cattails that ringed the marsh.

I crouched and, using the vegetation as a shield, worked my way deeper into the pond. Individual swans began drifting in and out of the blur in front of me. I reached the last clump of cattails unseen, the water a few inches from the top of my boots. I bent low and remained motionless, my cap and shoulders now white with a fresh coating of snow.

Swans moved in and out in front of me like giant ghosts. Their long necks arched over their backs or dipped into the water. Their heads would reappear with strands of dripping pondweed dangling from their black and orange bills. Sometimes they tipped on end with their rumps pointing skyward and their webbed feet waving above the waterline like black flags.

The swans moved through my field of view singly or in groups of two or three, sometimes no more than a few feet from my hiding spot. They were absolutely silent. The only sound was the murmur of snow striking the water's surface.

I watched for a long time, until my cramped body ached and my legs began to numb through my thin rubber boots. Reluctantly, I freed my feet from the muck, crept back to shore, and walked back to my house through the soft storm.

A Cat And A Brother

Cats were born, lived out their several lives, and disappeared, mostly unnamed and unremembered. Ira, a big gray tiger, was the exception. For some reason he attached himself to me, following me around and rubbing against my leg. If the truth is known, I became attached to him as well.

A row of small doors extended up the front of our silo. A metal chute wrapped around the doors, allowing silage to be thrown down to a waiting wagon. In the evening, sparrows would fly up or down the chute and roost on the wooden cross-braces that held the doors in place.

Ira learned to climb up the chute and catch the sleeping sparrows. One morning I came out of the house and heard a cat yowling. Ira was stuck. He was peering over the top of the chute and was afraid to move. I climbed up and attempted to rescue him, but he was so terrified that he bit and scratched at me when I tried to dislodge him.

I returned to the ground and unrolled a long string from a roll of baling twine. I climbed back to Ira and looped and tied the twine around his torso, just behind his front legs. Holding on high above his back, so he couldn't bite me, I quickly pulled him up and away from his death grip and swung him out into space. If you think he was yowling before, you should have heard him now. I hand-over-handed the squirming, struggling cat to the ground and hurried down and carefully released him.

Nobody ever accused Ira of being a fast learner; a few days later he was back on his perch at the top of the silo. Luckily I still had the string. I climbed up and repeated the process. This time the lesson stuck. He either learned to stay out of the chute or learned to climb down by himself.

Ira came to an unfortunate and improbable end. We had both reached the age where we liked to run around. I was coming home late one night when, about a mile south of our farm, a gray tiger cat suddenly ran across the road in front of my car.

Ira wasn't the only one in our family who climbed silos.

My brother Arlo was about three when Marlys and I decided he was old enough for his first climbing adventure. With me in front to pull and Mar behind to push and catch, we started up the chute. We had just reached the top and were all looking over the chute when my dad came out of the house. He was very calm. "Don't anyone move." He quickly climbed up and carried Arlo to safety.

I'm glad I didn't have to go down and get a twine string.

I'm sure Arlo was as well.

Fishing

A good day of fishing involved tying my Zebco rod and reel to my handlebars, riding three miles to Fedge Lake, casting a blob of worms into the algae-greened water, and dragging out a mess of slimy bullheads. My catch, threaded on a twine stringer, joined my fishing gear on the handlebars. The fish were dry and brittle by the time I reached home but amazingly, still alive. I nailed their heads to the edge of our hayrack and pulled off their tough, scale-less skin with a pair of pliers. Gutted and decapitated, they were thrown into a pan of water and taken in the house for a gourmet dinner.

Fishing was about to get a whole lot better.

We visited my mom's relatives in Hancock, Minnesota several times a year, alternating our stays between her sisters' families. We were staying with my Uncle Bob and Aunt Helen on this trip. The second day we were there, my Cousin Richie asked if I wanted to go fishing; they had been catching Northerns in a small stream near their farm. We ignored a dark storm cloud building in the west, packed our gear, and headed down the gravel road.

"Small stream" had been an overstatement; it looked as though, with a running start, I could jump to the far side. We approached a narrow bridge and pulled onto the shoulder. Swirling currents had carved out a pond on one side of the road.

The western sky was absolutely black. Lightning had sharpened to jagged bolts and the thunder was no longer a rumble but a series of continuous crashes. The hot air was completely still and charged with electricity.

Hurrying through the ditch, we made our first casts, being careful to keep them short so our spoons didn't land on the opposite shore. Wham! Wham! I can't say who caught what or when. It was an absolute frenzy. The lures were struck instantly and continuously; sometimes they hooked a fish and sometimes they were sent flying harmlessly into the air. Sometimes a Northern would frantically hit a lure three or four times as we reeled in. One big fish leaped from the water, desperately trying to catch my spoon as I raised it from the water to recast.

The storm was almost on us; a dark wall of water raced across the field. We kept casting and hollering as the action continued and the number of wiggling fish in the grass behind us grew.

Then it hit. We were instantly soaked; seeing became difficult as water flooded our eyes and ran down our faces. The downpour made the pond boil and roar. Noah would have been impressed.

The fish stopped biting.

We fished on, driven by our excitement. The pond was still full of Northerns, but ten minutes of futile casting later, we surrendered. We threw our rods and our catch into the trunk and, drenched, drove home through the storm.

Lloyd's Barn

Lloyd Biisser and my dad grew up on neighboring farms. They were cousins and lifetime friends. Lloyd would today be categorized as a concrete sequential; all things on his farm were kept neat and orderly. His tools and machinery were aligned in rows, his animals brushed and clean, and his barn immaculate. He had a phobia of barn fires.

We regularly drove our Case tractor with its mounted loader into our barn, often spending hours removing cattle manure. I don't ever remember Dad worrying that the exhaust stack might be a fire hazard. Lloyd, on the other hand, was paranoid; he stored his tractor in his barn but never drove it in or out. The tractor was always shut off and rolled in and out manually or with his team of horses.

A few years ago I discovered the cause of his concern. I was looking through some pictures from my Uncle John's album and discovered one labeled "Biisser's barn fire." The photo, taken about 1915, shows the building engulfed in flames. Horse harnesses, pulled from the barn, lay in piles just out of harm's way. Lloyd had been about twenty when his dad's barn was destroyed.

Here lies the supreme irony: after Lloyd's death, the new owner drove a tractor into the barn. Sparks from its exhaust ignited the ceiling. The fire spread throughout the building, burning it to the ground.

Lloyd's barn, in spite of its outwardly impeccable appearance, held a dark secret. My father and I were working outside one day when he suddenly paused; something in our conversation had triggered his memory. Dad was not normally much of a talker, but I could see from his expression he was about to tell me something he considered important. I think the following story was meant to be instructional as well as informational.

Lloyd had a young hired man who was working in the haymow, moving hay from a large pile in the center of the barn and forking it through a row of holes into the mangers below. It was a job he had done many times. He would throw hay down each hole, drop his fork down one hole, jump down another to the soft hay below, push the hungry animals out of the way, and spread the hay in the mangers.

This day was no different; he finished his task, dropped his fork tines first into the hay, and moved to the next hole, preparing to jump. Something distracted him, perhaps a cat or birds flying around in the cupola. He paused. Investigated. He returned to the hole and jumped. He jumped down the wrong hole.

The fork had entered the hay and stopped in an absolutely vertical position. His body struck the fork in perfect alignment. His weight drove the fork downward through the hay until the tines reached the solid floor of the manger. The sudden terrible jolt ripped a hole in his overalls and drove the rounded end of the handle through his rectum and deep into his intestines.

The next horrifying minutes are lost to history but not to the imagination.

He was rushed to the doctor in Madelia. "Don't bother doing anything for me, Doc; I know I am going to die."

A few days later he died.

Opening Day

If I hadn't seen it in person I wouldn't have believed it. There was no place to park. Main Street and all the adjacent side streets were packed with hunters. You could tell they were from the city. They had it all: fancy Red Wing boots and new canvas pants and coats with matching caps. Pink-tongued dogs, dripping saliva, stuck their heads out half-opened windows or lounged in big crates in the back of station wagons. Cafes and hardware stores overflowed. It was opening day.

I was fifteen the year I fell through the ice. I had been hunting muskrats along the west shore of Wilson's Lake; one minute I was shuffling along above a swimming rat and the next I was waist deep in icy water. It was a long walk to the pickup. A day or two later, Dr. Boysen put me in the hospital. It was the opening weekend of pheasant hunting. I had pneumonia.

The spectacle outside my window began to temper my feelings of self-pity. 1955 was the beginning of a major revolution in the American automobile. The latest models had been out for a few weeks. They were beauties. They had new grills and new two-tone profiles, their bright colors separated by crazy chrome styling. Everything about the '55s was new and different. Spectacular Chevys, Fords, DeSotos, Packards, and Pontiacs were scattered among the mundane cars of yesteryear. Backed up by the stop sign at the junction of Highways 60 and 15, they had stopped or were creeping along, showing off in front of my hospital window. It wasn't such a bad opening day after all.

Running Underwater

It took me a long time to learn to swim, especially above water. My high-density, no-fat body was poorly adapted to surface swimming. I was a freshman before I found the motivation and the tools for success. My friends had begun swimming out to the raft. Not wanting to be left behind, I bought a pair of rubber swim fins. Eventually I learned to swim to the raft unaided, although in the first few attempts the outcome seemed very much in doubt.

I was wading in waist-deep water when my toe struck a rock. I ducked under and came up holding a twenty-pound, erosion-smoothed boulder. Struck by a rare burst of creativity, I clutched the stone to my chest, took a deep breath, stretched myself out horizontally underwater and began running along the bottom of Fedge Lake. The bottom was just the right consistency of mud and sand to give my toes the grip needed to propel myself forward. With a little practice, I was soon moving at high speed and for amazing distances under the murky water.

Never shy about making myself the center of attention, I hatched a scheme to do just that. I transported the rock and placed it on the muddy bottom along one side of the raft. The next time a group of us were fooling around on the raft, I began to brag about my amazing ability to swim underwater, pointing out a distance far from the raft that I would be able to reach. A challenge was offered and of course accepted. I took a deep breath and dived in the direction I had pointed. I quickly reversed my direction and swam to the rock, grabbed it to my chest and began to run. I ran and ran, continuing until I thought my lungs would burst, then dropped the rock and shot to the surface. To my surprise I had exceeded the mark I had set.

I returned to the raft to bask in my newfound glory. "I can make it a lot further than that," I bragged. The skeptics once again reared their ugly heads. Making a big production of filling my lungs, I dived away from the raft. I had no rock to pick up but my plan didn't require one. I turned underwater and swam around to the backside of the raft. I surfaced and quietly swam to the ladder and waited.

Above, I could hear the conversations of my increasingly nervous friends as they stared intently down the lake. "How can he hold his breath so long?" "I hope he's okay." "How can he go so far?" At the optimal moment I stuck my head over the back of the raft.

"He's probably running."

Krajewski For President

It's difficult to defeat an incumbent war hero. The Democratic Party was prepared to give it their best shot, running Adlai Stevenson of Illinois, their repeat candidate from the 1952 election, against Dwight Eisenhower.

Suddenly a new candidate was added to the list of presidential hopefuls. New Jersey's Henry Krajewski was no "Johnny-come-lately" to presidential politics; he was repeating the bid he had made for that high office four years earlier. Mr. K. made an immediate splash on the national scene with his catchy entrance into the race. He arrived at his county courthouse with a pig under one arm and a signed petition in hand. The signatures were mandatory, the pig optional. He was a candidate for president.

Madelia's senior social studies class organized a mock campaign and election. Imagine the horror my friends and I experienced when we discovered that all the campaign literature being posted was for Stevenson and Eisenhower. We naturally stepped up to assist Krajewski in his election bid. 1956 would be his year.

I feel it my duty to inform you that Henry did not emerge victorious. I place the blame squarely on old-fashioned dirty politics. The senior-led bias proved too difficult to overcome. Krajewski's campaign was neither given representation at the convention nor was his name included on the ballot.

It was difficult finding the particulars of Mr. Krajewski's platform. We had no Internet and the national press was no help; they even failed to inform us of his rational for selecting the pig as his party symbol. Only later, when it was too late, did we discover the famous motto that would have pushed him over the top: "The Democrats have been hogging the Administration at Washington for twenty years and it's about time the people began to squeal."

Undeterred by the lack of specifics, we hammered out a supporting platform complete with a catchy slogan: "Krajewski, he's the slob for the job." The groundwork having been laid, we burned the midnight oil, attempting to match Eisenhower and Stevenson poster for poster. The placement of campaign literature can be critical.

Our key ineffective move was to sneak into the school, drag out the tall ladder the janitors used to replace light bulbs, and tape posters to the high ceiling in the main hall.

The opposition worked to thwart us at every turn, even going so far as to call our campaign "frivolous." Undaunted, we carried on, certain of eventual victory.

Students can be such sheep. Henry Krajewski garnered one vote.

Roadboarding

I can roadboard twelve miles an hour. I know this because that was our Case tractor's top speed.

Roadboarding is a relatively unknown sport, developed in the mid-fifties. It is unknown because I invented it and, as far as I know, was the only one to ever participate. This sport, while neither cerebral nor competitive, does hold its share of minor thrills.

Baling hay was hard work but had a certain amount of downtime, especially the trips back and forth from the field to the farm. To add a little excitement to these journeys, I built a roadboard. This piece of athletic equipment is built from a three-foot-long, one-by-twelve board. Holes are drilled through each of the front corners and through the front center. One end of a fifteen-foot rope is tied to the center hole and the other end to the back of the hayrack. Three-foot-long ropes are threaded through the corner holes and tied to a section of broomstick. "She's ready to go."

I make sure the long rope is fully extended to avoid a sudden jerk when the tractor starts out. The rig starts slowly at first, but once the road is reached and the throttle opened, we accelerate to full speed. By shifting my weight from side-to-side and pulling unevenly on the handle, I can cause the board to swing back and forth behind the rack as it bounces and slides on the rough gravel. It's possible to board backwards and make spins in the air.

Mishaps occur; spills are part of the game. Recovering from an accident requires the boarder to run at least thirteen miles an hour. Dad certainly wasn't going to slow down for such "damn foolishness."

WALLY

Wally Klatt sat next to me in the back row of my social studies class. Each day he would carefully stack his books on top of a big three-ring binder and, when the bell rang, scuttle out the door. A couple minutes later, as I walked into Mr. Brandt's agriculture classroom, Wally would invariably comment, "Ha, I beat you."

One day I found an empty notebook on the floor next to my desk. I carefully freed the wire spiral from the cover and stretched it to its full length. Near the end of the hour, I tied one end of the wire to the leg of my desk and, as he watched the second hand, tied the other to the little hole in the zipper of Wally's binder.

The bell rang on cue, and Wally snatched up his tall stack of books and rushed for the door.

The wire from a spiral notebook is four feet long.

The stack of books seemed to explode. I walked over the disaster and out the door.

A few minutes later a decidedly rattled Wally walked into Mr. Brandt's room.

Smiling, I ignored his angry glare.

"Ha, I beat you."

Accident

I pictured myself a comedian and used humor to draw attention to myself whenever possible.

My Cousin Sherwood was on leave from the army and had been staying out late with his friends. One afternoon he agreed to take Marlys and me swimming at the beach in Starbuck. We stopped at a gas station near my Aunt Olga's house and, while Sherwood filled the car, I went inside and bought a bottle of Coca-Cola. I heard a honk and placed the half-finished bottle on the counter and hurried to the car.

On the north edge of Hancock, we rolled through the stop sign and turned northwest onto Highway 9. I watched as the insect-spattered grille of a bronze 1950 Ford struck my passenger-side door.

Strangers were running excitedly around in the ditch between the smashed cars. We were transported to the hospital in Morris. I remember making an absolutely hilarious comment as the doctor sewed up a long cut on the top of my head. He obviously had no sense of humor. I heard him whisper to the nurse, "I think we better admit him."

A sentiment often shared by those who knew me.

Sherwood and I were released the next day; luckily no one was seriously injured.

I never leave a soda unfinished.

A Brush With Stardom

Madelia celebrated its centennial in 1957. The town went all out to make this a great celebration. There was a spectacular fireworks display, a mile-long parade, an open house at each of the schools, and a grand pageant depicting the history of Madelia from Pre-Columbian times to the present. The pageant, with its cast of thousands, was desperate for participants. Fourteen boys from my class and the class ahead of me were drafted to serve in Napoleon's Grande Armée. Our role was to participate in a depiction of France's sale of the Louisiana Purchase to America.

Soldiers march and stand at attention. They do not speak unless spoken to, thus my opportunities for thespian honors were limited. Our little band of soldiers was to march on stage in columns of two, stand at attention during the requisite speeches and document signings, then exit, stage left, with our best martial bearing.

A large stage was constructed on the baseball outfield at Watona Park. Spectators could sit in the provided bleacher seats and benches or bring their own chairs. Standing room extended all the way to the river.

Rehearsal and the Friday evening performance were carried off without a hitch. We donned our three-pointed hats, shouldered our long-staffed French flags, and marched on and off stage with military precision.

Saturday's matinee would be played to a packed park, with the performance starting at two o'clock. I knew the Napoleon segment was scheduled to begin thirty minutes into the show. There was no reason to waste time backstage, not when the pool hall was open.

The pool hall was nearly empty; there was just Vern on his stool by the bar and Earl Smith and I playing snooker. Everyone else was at the pageant. I kept one eye on the clock and the other on Earl. There was plenty of time; it took fifteen minutes at most to get to the park.

Snooker is an unpredictable sport. Scratches, defensive play, and missed shots can all increase the time it takes to complete a game. I could see that time was becoming a factor but, if I left early, I would be admitting defeat and be forced to pay for the game. The faster I played, the more shots I missed. I don't remember who won. At two fifteen I rushed out the door and jumped into my car. Who would have thought there would still be heavy traffic now that the pageant had begun?

I abandoned my car at the park's entrance and raced across the ball field. Napoleon's men were standing in the wings with their flags raised. The forward march command had been given. The small army could see me racing across the field. Good soldiers never abandon one of their own; the men began marching in place. I ran up the stage steps to the flag barrel. All that remained was a broken, flagless stick.

The show must go on. The soldiers forward-marched and performed admirably in spite of the gaping hole in their ranks.

The only review I received from this, my first and only dabble into the performing arts, was in the form of a threatening question from a particularly irate critic: my mother.

"Where were you?"

Alfred E. Newman

I had exhausted most of the easy classes by the time I registered for my senior year.

Typing looked like the best bet.

My friend Dave Erickson and I walked into the typing room the first day of school and selected our seats. The room was filled with mostly sophomore and junior girls, a detail that did not escape our attention. Soon Mr. Forseth, a young, first-year teacher, entered the classroom and, with forced confidence, called us to attention. After a short introduction of himself and the curriculum, he passed a sheet of paper around the room and asked us to sign our names. The paper went up and down the rows until it reached my desk. I added my name and, before passing the sheet to Dave, noticed an extra wide space between two girls' signatures. I carefully inserted Alfred E. Newman's name.

Mr. Forseth, like any good teacher, was anxious to associate names with faces; calling students by their names is a time-honored method of forming a teacher-student bond. Mr. Forseth read each name and, as the student raised their hand, commented or smiled before moving on to the next.

"Alfred E. Newman."

The class looked around, expecting to see a new student.

"Alfred E. Newman?"

Giggles and whispers.

The Jekyll to Hyde transformation was instantaneous. Mr. Forseth's face flushed and twisted. The girl above Alfred's name was verbally dragged to one corner of the room and the girl below his name to the opposite. The class sat in silent shock.

Some teachers have a very poor sense of humor.

The Nun

A plan was hatched in December of 1957. Four senior friends and I would take a road trip to California over Christmas vacation. My parents reluctantly agreed, with one stipulation: no night driving.

A sock hop was planned for the night following the last day of classes. We couldn't leave right after school and miss something that important. We would leave early the following morning; the hop would be a great place to showcase our big adventure. Wait, what if we impressed everyone even more and left directly from the dance?

Darwyn's red 1953 Chevy convertible was parked in front of the school. The designated hour, one that had been skillfully promoted, finally arrived. The five of us walked casually across the dance floor and down the hall to the car.

Five miles later we made our first stop, the Five-Mile Corner. This little sin city consisted of three bars at a road junction south of town. None of us had ever been there before. The stop was a short one: five packs of cigarettes, five lighters, and we were off.

Our plan was to camp when needed and mooch from relatives when possible. Each day was filled with high adventure. Not intending this to become a travelogue, I will go directly to the subject. We were driving west through Arizona at fifty-five miles an hour. I know this because there were cacti and because Darwyn wouldn't let us drive his car any faster.

1957 was the heyday of the American automobile. Each fall, companies competed to release the most stylish, modern-looking vehicles. Engines and fins were growing and chrome and two-tone paint the rage. Arguments and discussions, usually Chevy versus Ford, occupied our days.

The car ahead was traveling fifty-four miles an hour. We had plenty of time to look it over as we inched past. It was so nondescript that it caught our eye: a plain, all-black, low-priced '55 Chevy. The driver edged into view, a plain nondescript lady in plain, nondescript clothes. Elbows nudged ribs. We subtly turned and stared and, when she looked back, we turned away.

"Did you see that?"

"She must be a nun."

"You think so?"

"Did you see those plain clothes?"

"And how about that car?"

"Yeah, she had to have been."

We continued down the freeway, ten or twenty miles later coming to the California border and check station. We pulled into a space and began answering the officer's questions. We were here for a vacation. We had no fruits or vegetables. We'd be staying about a week.

The lady in the black Chevy pulled into the space next to us. More nudges and more, now slightly-sheepish, stares. She looked our way as we pulled forward. We shared a few more jokes but soon forgot about the lady and her car; we had more exciting fish to fry. We were in California.

We were getting hungry. An hour or so later we pulled into a truck stop for a quick meal; we were in a hurry. We were walking back to our car just as the lady pulled in and parked. We had more fun laughing and discussing the strange series of coincidences; this would certainly be a good story to tell when we got home.

It was my turn to drive. There were no freeways in Minnesota; this was my first experience. Driving was fun at first but I became more and more nervous as the traffic increased and the Coastal Range loomed ahead. I had also never driven in mountains. We suddenly burst over a final ridge and there, sprawled before us, was San Diego. The two lanes going in our direction quickly expanded to three, then four, and finally five. Speed limits went unheeded; squeezed between bumpers, I was carried along at seventy-five miles an hour. We were looking for the suburb of Lemon Grove but no one knew where it was or where we were.

My armpits were sweating and my knuckles turning white as I worked my way to the right lane and drove down the first exit ramp we came to. I turned left at the stop sign, drove under the freeway, turned right on a residential street, and pulled over to the curb. Someone else could drive. We piled out of the car and spread our map across the hood.

A black 1955 Chevy drove past and pulled into the driveway next to us. A lady opened the trunk, removed her suitcase, and walked toward the house. Now everyone, including the nun, was blatantly staring. Here was an opportunity to say hello, tell her where we were from, and joke and laugh about the strange series of events. Nobody said a word. She walked past us into the house. We got back into our car and drove away.

I sometimes imagine the story as told to her friends. "You'll never believe what happened. I was driving through Arizona and this carload of cool, good-looking guys pulled up beside me and began checking me out . . ."

Sputnik

The Soviets launched Sputnik, the first artificial Earth satellite, in early October 1957. The fear and uncertainty spread by that event was to have far-reaching repercussions and responses for our country. The United States government poured money into the development of its rocket program and into all levels of science education. American media, as they often do, was quick to spread information, whether fact or fiction.

Many American students were drilled in the protective technique of diving under their desks and shielding their heads with their arms. Madelia students were drilled in spelling and multiplication tables. Aside from some discussion in my social studies classes, the only memories I have of the event are ones of curiosity.

A few days after Sputnik was launched, a rumor spread that the bass were biting at Fox Lake, near Sherburn, thirty miles to the southwest. Richard Ellingsberg and I loaded my family's old aluminum boat and three-and-a-half-horsepower Mercury motor into the back of our pickup. We left early, at four in the morning, wanting to be on the lake at sunrise.

Richard was an avid newspaper reader. American astronomers had recently observed and mapped Sputnik's orbit; Richard came armed with the necessary information. We pulled onto the shoulder a few miles south of St. James and stood next to the road, staring east. Richard glanced back and forth from the sky to his watch. There it was, right on time, a small, wondrous, star-like object threading its way through the early morning constellations. We watched for several minutes as it passed slowly overhead and faded in the western sky.

Our boat was launched from the Fox Lake pavilion's parking lot. We fished for several hours, employing all the latest techniques and equipment. Eventually, with the sun beating down and fatigue setting in, we returned to the dock empty-handed.

An old man in faded bib overalls was sitting in the shade alongside the dock; next to him was a Folger's can of worms and, in the water in front of him, a nice stringer of bass.

Our consolation prize was lifetime membership in the "I saw Sputnik" club.

Grand Canyon

My friends and I were returning from a Christmas vacation road trip to California. We had behaved admirably for the entire ten days and, in spite of being sorely tempted in Tijuana, were returning with our honor and our reputations intact.

We left California on New Year's Day and arrived at the South Rim of the Grand Canyon just before dark. Camping regulations must have been more relaxed than they are today. We pulled into a nearly empty parking lot next to a cluster of park buildings and set up our tents on the lawn a short distance from the canyon.

January second dawned cold and clear, far below freezing. We emerged from our tents and watched as the bright morning sun lifted behind us and painted the far canyon wall with ribbons of muted color.

A rustic park sign announced, "Canyon Floor, Seven Miles." We cautiously stepped forward and looked down; an impossibly steep series of switchbacks descended and disappeared along the canyon wall. We held a conference. The little restaurant a short distance away was still closed and, besides, it would be a shame to visit the Grand Canyon and not walk at least part of the way down.

This was fun. Every few hundred feet the sharply descending trail cut back on itself, revealing both where we had been and where we were going. The textures and colors of the sandstone, shale, and limestone layers continued to change as we descended ever deeper into the plateau and into the past. Rock squirrels and chipmunks chattered and eyed us suspiciously from their perches and crevasses among the rock piles and talus.

We looked up. It was a long way to the top; we must have been walking for a couple of hours. The strange braking gait we were forced to use was beginning to burn our thighs, and we were getting hungry and thirsty. Just as we were about to turn back we came upon a sign advertising a restaurant at the bottom of the canyon. That wouldn't be so bad; we were already halfway down. We could eat a relaxed breakfast and rest before returning to the top.

The Colorado River was narrow and shallow and turned out to be a disappointment. We threw a few stones to the far side and looked expectantly up and down the river. There was no eating establishment in sight, only a small sign informing us that the restaurant was three miles upstream. We did the math. It was seven miles down so it must be seven miles back up; another three miles to the restaurant and back would bring the total to twenty miles. What if the restaurant was closed?

We eyed the brown water. Was it safe to drink? We decided not to take a chance and reluctantly began the long hike back to the rim. Far above we could see a miniature mule train making its way slowly down the switchbacks. The sun was now high and the dry desert air grew warmer. The upward trek began to tax a whole new set of muscles. Seven miles uphill is a far longer distance than seven miles down. Rest breaks became more frequent and our group gradually began to split up, the order of ascent based on the fitness level of each member.

The line of mules passed us on the left, hugging the canyon wall. The swaying riders nodded or gave us a short cheerful greeting. I don't think we ever considered the danger we were in. We could have asked for water.

We passed the "restaurant at the bottom" sign. It was hard to know if this single landmark was a blessing or a curse. Our legs became heavier and our rest stops more frequent, even though we understood that the more we rested the longer it would take us to get to the rim.

It was well after noon when we finally straggled to the top. At least the restaurant was open and they sold malted milks. We drank water and sucked down ice cream until we could hold no more.

We had to get on the road; our adventure had put us far behind schedule. We were getting into the car when Darwyn's leg suddenly began to cramp. He pulled himself erect and struggled to relax his hamstring. The next half hour was crazy. Every few miles someone would holler and grab one of his legs. Sometimes the cramp could be relaxed in the car but othertimes we had to pull onto the shoulder and let the afflicted party walk it off. We learned that cold ice cream and fatigued muscles make a poor combination.

I recently read an article stating that the National Park Service recommends hikers bring along plenty of food and water, and under no circumstances should they attempt to walk both up and down the Grand Canyon on the same day. I'm sure they never imagined having to caution anyone not to walk to the bottom and back before breakfast and without water.

California Cool. Left to Right: Royce, Jim, Erling and me. Darwyn is on the driver's side.

WHAT I LEARNED IN SCHOOL

Considering I attended the Madelia Public Schools for thirteen years, the list of the things I learned is relatively short. It appears that embarrassment and humiliation were near the top.

Like most of my classmates in first grade, I owned an eight pack of Crayola color crayons. Lance James, who sat in the desk across the aisle from me, possessed a four-layered, ascending-level, thirty-two pack. I was humbled and awed by his collection of colors, which included red-violet, cerulean, blue-green, indigo, and the now socially unacceptable "flesh." Lance was rightfully proud of the status his crayons provided.

One warm spring afternoon, the bell in the hall outside our first-floor room began clanging unceasingly. We all stared at each other in wonderment. Mrs. Lord calmly took charge. "This is a fire drill, it is just for practice, no one is in danger. Leave everything on your desk, line up in a row, and follow me out of the school. Don't stop moving until I tell you to stop."

Just in case Mrs. Lord wasn't telling the truth, Lance grabbed his box of crayons. We marched through the hall, down the long row of cement steps, and across the schoolyard, accompanied by the incessant ringing. We milled around on the lawn for a long time. Finally the bell stopped ringing and, after some amount of confusion on the part of our teachers, we were herded back to our rooms. Lance let out a cry. Most of his color crayons were missing; during the bedlam on the lawn, he had been holding his box sideways.

Mrs. Lord didn't panic. She calmly sent Lance, with me as his assistant, back to the playground to search for his lost crayons. Lance hadn't remained stationary during the long drill and his crayons were scattered across a wide area. We eventually found all but two. Lance, with his concrete sequential personality, was especially crushed by the fact that one of his favorites had been stepped on and now wiggled loosely within its paper wrapper. I, on the other hand, was rightfully proud of the role I had played in the rescue.

———

*Marlys and me on my first day of school.
I remember the sun was so bright I had difficulty looking at the camera.*

Poet Helen Hunt Jackson, in the mid-1800s, penned an autumn favorite, "September." It begins, "The goldenrod is yellow; the corn is turning brown; the trees in apple orchards with fruit are bending down." Mrs. Nestrud, our third-grade teacher, as part of a quest to instill in us a small amount of culture, required that we memorize the first few verses. When asked who knew the first verse, I confidently raised my hand. At Mrs. Nestrud's request, I began: "The goldenrod is yellow; the corn is bending down…" The class began laughing uproariously. Their response, even to this day, seems excessive. My face became hot and turned beet red. Mrs. Nestrud, bless her, tried to shield me from my embarrassment by making a joke about how the winds had been strong lately and had indeed been having that effect on the corn. One would think the lesson learned from this experience would be: don't raise your hand.

Mrs. Nestrud asked: could a brother and sister be identical twins?

My reasoning went something like this: some mixed-sex siblings look a lot alike. If they look really a lot alike, couldn't they be considered identical? Once again my hand shot up and once again the results were the same. Evidently there was more to being identical than facial similarity.

One day in Mrs. Jensen's fourth grade class, we had a visitor. Stern and formal, she had been sent by the Department of Education to evaluate our elementary teachers. The class had been given a writing assignment. As we wrote, the lady wandered up and down the rows, carefully watching our progress. When we finished our task, the visitor stepped to the front of the room and asked for our attention. She had observed someone who had wonderful penmanship and wanted to recognize that person for his excellence. She walked down my row, stopped at my desk, and looked down at my paper. She uttered a soft, shocked "oh," and then muttered, almost to herself, "This isn't him." She recovered quickly, looked around, and held up Lance's paper. Fame is fleeting.

Mr. Parker was one of my seventh-grade teachers. He was a good teacher and a very nice man. The last day before Christmas, we had a small party near the end of our class period. We were going to play a game. We were supposed to identify the person he was drawing on the board. He drew a very round stick figure and everyone laughed and said, "Bill." Next he drew a figure of a boy with huge ears. Again the class laughed and said, "Wayne." Even nice teachers can make poor decisions.

My sophomore year turned out to be a critical one for my education. I had a study hall in the library. My table was located next to the stacks. When I wasn't shooting craps with Dave Erickson, I would pull a book from the shelf near to my table. By chance, I was seated next to the school's complete supply of bird books and spent hours looking at the pictures and reading the captions. Several years later, when I was a sophomore in college, I chanced to take a class in ornithology and surprised everyone, including myself, by identifying all the birds. I received a rare A in the class and went on to develop a lifelong passion for birds and birding.

Mr. Schuldheiz's history class was quite interesting and easy to do well in if you studied your notes before a test. This was a moot point as I often didn't get around to taking notes. I looked forward to his class for the competition. Mr. Schuldheiz had the habit of using two phrases during his lectures: "and so to speak" and "and so on and so forth." At the beginning of each class, Richard Ellingsberg, who sat alphabetically to my left, and I would alternate having first choice. The bet was a nickel a day. Richard kept a chart in his notebook and, when one of the phrases was used, placed a check in the appropriate column. I don't know if the bets were ever paid but, as with any good contest, it was more about the competition and sportsmanship than about wins and losses.

The first few days I was in Mr. Rommel's English class he expected that I would turn out to be a good student, foolishly thinking I would be like my older sister, Marlys. He was soon embarrassed and a little disappointed by his assumption. My area of expertise was reading books. Not being good at multitasking, I chose to concentrate on my reading and ignore what was going on in class. Mr. Rommel usually ignored me as well, but one day, seeing I was again oblivious to his teaching, asked a question and said, "Mr. Feder, can you answer that?" The class turned and looked at me, eager to hear my response. Everyone knew I didn't know the question. I now suspect it may have had something to do with the parts of speech. Seeing I was in a bind, my friend Dick Blue leaned in my direction and whispered, "Shakespeare." In my heart, I knew this was the wrong answer, but I was unable to think of anything better. "Shakespeare." The class burst out laughing and even the staid Mr. Rommel got a small smirk on his face.

It is important to learn from one's mistakes. I think I only fell for Dick's trick two more times that semester.

Bulldozers

It was one of my last trips to my Uncle Frank and Aunt Florence's farm. I walked past the abandoned outhouse and into the windbreak west of the buildings. Near the far side, a partially obscured network of roads and highways branched and twisted through the weeds and duff.

The rotting two-by-four bulldozers were parked in uneven rows or scattered across the ground, partially buried and tilted at impossible angles.

We had piled from our car those years ago, where Sherwood stood waiting. "I have something to show you." He hurried me into the woods where the construction project was underway, proudly showing me his newly-made road equipment. We bladed the soft loam, digging deep ditches and packing the raised roadbeds. We played until dark.

I didn't see Sherwood much anymore; he had graduated, gone off to join the Army.

I stood for a long time in the dark woods. I missed him.

I was sad we had grown too old.

JACKRABBITS

Jackrabbits are actually hares; their babies, unlike true rabbits which are born naked and helpless, are covered with hair and able to hop and move around at birth. Female jackrabbits hide their camouflaged babies in separate shallow, individual depressions and return several times each day to nurse. This is a good example of nature not putting all of its eggs, or in this case, hares, in one basket.

Nature sometimes gets out of balance. The winter of my junior year, a combination of ecological factors including birthrate, food supply, and predator pressure resulted in an explosion of the jackrabbit population.

Sunday afternoons I would take my 22 to Richard's. One of us would circle through the cattail and willow marsh north of his farm and drive the resident herd across the township road and into the snow-packed field to the west. Territorial boundaries were finite. The rabbits followed the mostly submerged fence line a quarter mile, then turned south for a half mile, before again turning left and dispersing in the woods and pasture lands surrounding Fedge Lake. The next Sunday they would be back in the marsh, waiting for us.

This predictable route allowed the non-driving partner to wait in ambush as the rabbits streamed past or sat up on hind legs to look back for their pursuer. It was legal to sell jackrabbits. At fifty cents a rabbit, sold as mink food, it was easy to calculate the fortune waiting to be harvested. Fortunately for the rabbits, our marksmanship left much to be desired and allowed most of the rabbits to survive the winter unscathed.

There was no surviving the dredge and the plow. Loss of grassland habitat, brought on by changing agricultural practices and government farm programs, began devastating the jackrabbit population.

I haven't seen a jackrabbit in southern Minnesota for twenty years.

Running

"Let's run around the basement."

No wonder I had so few friends; my idea of a good time was running in a circle around our furnace. Turn left at the water faucet, continue left past the coal bin, and back to the steps. One lap. The object was to run until you could no longer continue. Tightening your belt as far as possible helped reduce side aches.

I liked to run because I was pretty good at it, an excuse people use for many of the things they do in life. My elementary school memories are filled with running activities: tag, football, tackle tag, and racing. Naturally, when I reached seventh grade, I talked my parents into letting me go out for track and field.

Track practice, as far as I could tell, was little more than semi-organized chaos. All the boys from grades seven through twelve were herded from the locker room into the gym. A large circle was formed and, after a series of strange stretches and gyrations, someone blew a whistle. Everyone stampeded around the basketball floor. Heels were stepped on and backs pushed; eventually, as breathing rates increased and the pace slowed, the whistle was blown again. Everyone walked. This run-walk cycle was repeated a few more times until suddenly, two basketballs were thrown out and all the big kids began playing half-court ball. I guessed practice was over. The few younger kids present watched for a while from the bleachers and then went home.

Small variations on this theme continued for a couple more weeks until one warm spring day it was announced we were going outside. We were instructed to run to the football field. Downhill, and only a few blocks away, this seemed like a simple task, but many of the older kids thought differently and, at best, alternated walking with running.

Perhaps at some level a plan was in motion, but not for my age group. For the next three years we were on our own. We wrestled, played tag, and high jumped. We tried our hand at the shot and discus, barely getting either past the end of our toes. We didn't hurdle. We had no hurdles. For that matter, we had no track. Sometimes we joined the upper classmen as they ran a prescribed number of laps around the football field; other times we just watched.

Occasionally the big kids were missing from practice; gone, I suppose, to a track meet, whatever that was. I had never seen a track, let alone a meet. I never challenged the system, never knew that somewhere junior high kids might actually be competing. I remember one day when I was a freshman, the senior high milers were participating in a time trial. I joined in and finished second, a few yards behind the school's number one miler. No one was impressed; the first, third, and fourth place runners were entered in the next meet.

I was perfectly happy. I rarely missed practice; where else could one enjoy sanctioned fooling around such as this?

Things changed my sophomore year. Mr. Weihrauch became our new coach and began taking us to meets. God, I was scared. We went to Lake Crystal and ran under the lights; their track was an oval painted on grass. I ran the mile and finished in the middle of the pack. I had never been so tired in my life. I was often close to placing that season but usually came up just short. A total of five points was needed for a letter; the season ended and I had four and three-fourths. The season's final statistics were posted the last day of school. Mr. Weihrauch had rounded up. I was a letter winner, entitled to the jacket, the sweater, and all the accompanying honors and privileges I imagined were mine.

Mr. Nehowig became our new coach my junior year and greatly increased the number and quality of the meets we attended. Another change had taken place since the previous season: I had grown. The speed I had enjoyed in elementary school was gone but had luckily been replaced by endurance. I was certainly not a great runner but, over the next two seasons, won my share of races and broke all our school's distance records.

Coach Nehowig approached our group of distance runners shortly after school began my senior year. What did we think of forming a cross country team? Surprisingly, we ended the season just missing the regional championship by a few points. Richard Ellingsberg, our number three runner, injured his knee the night before the competition and was unable to compete. My friend Dave Erickson won the race, and we both qualified for, and placed quite high, in the state meet.

A running craze spread through Madelia High School my senior year. This craze, started by me, was not as universal as it might sound. My friends and I began running to out-of-town ballgames.

Dave and I had last hour study hall. Madelia was playing football at St. James. We decided to run to the game. We signed out to the restroom, went to the locker room, changed into our running clothes, and slipped out the side door. It was a simple plan: run the sixteen miles to their football field, watch the game, and catch a ride home. The problem turned out to be that we were too fit and arrived in St. James far too early. It was a hot day and we were becoming dehydrated. We entered the city limits and finally found a gas station, a place to buy a bottle of pop. Neither of us had brought along any money. We somehow found something to drink, money for the game, and a ride home. A few days later, Mr. Jansen, our superintendent, stopped us in the hall. He had been driving through Madelia the Friday before and had seen two kids running away from the school. Convinced that he was going to catch students skipping, he followed us. "Then I saw it was only you two."

The winter season arrived and Richard and I decided to run the twelve miles to a basketball game in Lake Crystal. I remember being absolutely exhausted when we reached the school, with the game already in progress. It was a sellout, standing room only. Richard and I sat on some cement steps in the lobby, too tired to watch.

It was sixteen miles to Truman and a very cold day. I talked Lance James into making the run with me. This was a hard one; I remember our running being interspersed with a lot of walking. It grew darker and colder and fans began passing us, heading for the game. Several pulled over, and the adults inside wanted to know if we were all right and if we wanted a ride. It was tempting.

The spring of my senior year, the region track meet was held in Windom. I was strong and confident; my qualifying time was the second fastest in the field. I knew I could make it to the state meet.

I still run the race in my mind. By the end of the first lap I was exhausted and by the third I had fallen from first to dead last. It was the slowest time I had run since my sophomore year. I was devastated. My running career was over and the last race of my life had ended in disaster.

Little did I know that in a few years I would be competing for Mankato State College and would continue running for twenty-five more years with the kids I coached on my high school track and cross country teams.

Dave and me in front of the high school the day before the State Cross Country Meet.

Water Skiing

The summer before my junior year, Jim Sorenson and I came across a deal that was too good to pass up. Buzzy Becker sold us his used fourteen-foot aluminum runabout and thirty-five horse Sea King motor for three hundred and fifty dollars. The price did not include gas, license, skis, life jackets, or doctor bills.

We learned to ski on two skis and drop off the non-slalom ski as we circled past the landing. Soon we could get up on one and, from then on, except when we were jumping, we never skied on two.

Our summer evenings and Sunday afternoons were filled. We sometimes skied on smaller lakes, but ten-mile-long Lake Hanska was our favorite. We skied for hours, tens of hours, hundreds of hours. We often took turns skiing the length of the lake and back.

I hear beginners bragging about skiing without falling, an unheard of occurrence in my world. A large percentage of my day was spent sliding, skidding, or bouncing across the top of the water at speeds in excess of forty miles an hour. If we weren't driving faster and cutting sharper, we considered it a waste of time.

Some people prefer to ride discs instead of skis. Jim showed up one day with a wooden stepladder and a supersized four-foot disc he had cut from a sheet of plywood. Best used on still, glass-smooth evenings, the goal was to get up on the disc, center the ladder, and climb as high as possible. The inevitable fall from near the top rung could be impressive.

I occasionally see water ski shows on television and notice that the participants use an L-shaped handle on their rope instead of the traditional bar-at-the-end-of-a-split-rope design. An observation too late made.

One day we were jumping on our homemade jump. Jim was driving. I slid up the jump and, I suppose showing off for maximum distance, lost my balance and began to fall. Not an uncommon occurrence. I let go of the rope as usual and dived for the water.

My left arm passed through the triangle formed by the handle and the two arms of the ski rope. The jerk from the speeding boat trapped my upper arm, and I was dragged underwater for several feet before the rope snapped. Observers said the boat was nearly brought to a stop and the front end lifted high above the water.

Jim hurried me to Madelia and notified Dr. Boysen, who met us at his office. My biceps muscle was flattened down to the bone, leaving an inch-deep groove in my upper arm. Dr. Boysen gave my arm a few exploratory wiggles, declared it unbroken, and placed it in a sling.

The sling was temporary. The indentation in my upper arm is permanent.

Ice Cream Cone

I wasn't involved in the beginning. We stopped on Main Street to talk with another carload of guys. They opened their trunk and showed us the prize: a three-foot-tall, glazed, paper mache ice cream cone, recently heisted from the marquee at Boom's Drive Inn. They were getting cold feet and wanted to dump the evidence.

"I'll take it."

We transferred the cone to my trunk.

What does one do with a three-foot ice cream cone? It waited patiently in my trunk for a few weeks. One day, we were water skiing on Lake Hanska, and I decided it was time to give the cone its first real adventure. I held it aloft as best I could, got up on the skis, and took her for a spin. We skied a mile or two down the lake and back before I released the rope and coasted to shore. The cone was only soggy in a few places.

A lot of people spend their Sundays at Lake Hanska. Who knew what had been seen? Maybe it was time to dispose of our trophy. You couldn't just throw it away; the cone deserved an honorable resting place.

When you come out of Vern's pool hall and look directly across Main Street, the first building that catches your eye is the Noonan Hotel, the tallest building in town. Several feet below the roof peak there is an eighteen-inch wide ledge.

It was a four-man operation. Wayne Nielsen, who worked part time for the Madelia Police Department, stood watch from the front steps of Vern's. This position would allow him to disclaim any involvement if we were busted. Paul Lickfett, Fred Joramo, the ice cream cone, and I went around to the back alley behind the hotel. Wooden stairs led to a small landing behind an apartment building. A simple step onto a railing, a short climb up a steep roof, and a series of boosts and pulls easily brought us to the roof of the Noonan. With one foot on either side of the peak, we crabbed our way to the Main Street end. A peek over the edge revealed a now-small Wayne casually pretending to ignore us. A look straight down disclosed that the distance from the peak to the ledge was greater than it had appeared from the ground.

A small can of tar and a flat stick emerged from somewhere, and a blob of sticky tar was smeared on the bottom of the cone. Wayne looked up and down Main Street and gave us the all-clear signal. One of us stretched down from the peak and lowered the cone toward the ledge. The bottom still had three feet to go. The cone was brought back to the roof and the mission reassessed.

"We won't drop you." I can tell they mean it and are trying hard not to, but when dangling upside down, far above a cement sidewalk, confidence tends to fade. I stretched my thirty-five-inch arms to their maximum, pushed the tarry bottom onto the ledge, and then expressed a sincere desire to be retrieved.

People in Madelia don't often look up. The cone settled in and for several days surveyed the town from its lofty position. It was finally spotted and reported to someone of importance. The fire department rushed to the scene and the hook and ladder crew brought it safely to earth.

It had been a bad crime week in Madelia. The Times Messenger reported the ice cream cone incident, along with another far less impressive petty crime, under the heading: "Vandals Strike."

The Cannon

Cannon are normally drawn by horses or trucks.

Madelia's World War I cannon hadn't budged from its cement pedestal in Flanders Park since the defeat of the dreaded Hun more than forty years earlier.

Our reasoning went something like this: the cannon and Madelia's students had coexisted for generations. Now that a new high school had been built, didn't this new wave of students deserve to continue that relationship? As a surprise gift we would deliver the gun to its new home, free of charge.

Paul and Fred were home from college for the summer. We parked our car a block away and, armed with Dad's bolt clipper, cautiously crossed the playground. We cut the chain that anchored the cannon and looked in all directions. Traffic was light after one in the morning.

We grasped the trail handles and lifted. It was heavier than we expected. It took two to hold the cannon vertical, leaving only one to push on the wheels, the best source of leverage.

Passing the log cabin, we turned left, up the slope toward the front of the high school gymnasium. That was as far as we got. The remaining half mile, although mostly downhill if we could get to the Catholic Church corner, seemed too daunting. We parked the cannon in the center of the intersection, pointed it west down the street toward the post office, and called it good enough.

Wayne Neilsen, our undercover informant, told us that when the police discovered the cannon the following morning, one of the wheels was within an inch of falling off the hub.

"Cannon topples, crushes vandal." Now there would have been a story to tell.

CULTIVATING

I don't hear very well. I maintain that mine is a chronic disorder, but my wife, Lynda, asserts that my problem is mostly selective.

Like most farm kids, I was anxious to learn to drive a tractor and help with the fieldwork, a misguided enthusiasm that I soon came to regret.

Some of our farming operations were short term or intermittent; cultivating corn and soybean fields was never-ending.

We had two cultivators: a two-row, mounted on our smaller SC Case, and a larger four-row on the DC. Cultivation began early in the growing season, shortly after the corn or beans emerged; if the competing weeds became too large, they were difficult to control. The first time over the field was a slow, tedious process; metal shields were suspended on either side of the rows to prevent dirt from being thrown over the small, delicate plants. I was quite old before Dad trusted me with this critical step.

We usually cultivated our fields four times throughout the growing season, finishing only when the crops became too tall to drive through, at which time the shade from the corn or beans was able to retard the growth of the surviving weeds. Usually there was only a few days break between the completion of one cycle and the beginning of the next.

I began cultivating with the small tractor when I was thirteen, but only for a few hours a day. It was difficult to learn to concentrate for long periods of time. Any lapse revealed itself by a long gap in the rows, one immediately and permanently displayed for my dad and our neighbors to see.

By the time I reached upper high school and beyond, I had moved up to the DC and was able and expected to work most of each day. Unfortunately, this period of my life corresponded closely with my habit of closing the pool hall each night at midnight. Blurry eyed from fatigue, dust, heat, and the sun's glare, I struggled to finish each day's work.

Some of our neighbors had radios mounted on the fenders of their tractors; Dad didn't believe in such foolishness. Except for a small transistor radio that crackled with each firing of the spark plugs, held to my ear on days the Twins played one of their rare afternoon games, diversion from boredom was left to me.

Singing was a staple. Far from prying ears, I unconsciously belted out and crooned the latest top ten hits. Chuck Berry, Buddy Holly, and Elvis never sounded better. It was only when I turned off the tractor and continued singing that my monotone, off-key performance became apparent.

Events in the natural world provided much of my entertainment. Small mammals – striped gophers, voles, and an occasional jumping mouse, with its long tail and kangaroo-like hind legs – ran, scurried, or hopped as they attempted to dodge or outrun the motorized monster bearing down on them.

One summer a kestrel haunted the edge of the eighty across the road from our farmstead. The small falcon would perch on the highline wires next to the road and, whenever it became hungry, fly to my tractor and follow me down the field. In a short time he would spot and capture a mouse or vole and carry it back to the wire. The bird would clasp and balance with one claw and, holding its prey in the other, tear open the mouse and devour it with its beak.

Killdeer nested in our fields. These little robin-sized shorebirds would scratch out a small hollow in the dirt and lay four or five black-flecked eggs. They became more and more excited with each round as I drew ever closer, dropping one wing and limping and fluttering, feigning injury in an attempt to lead me away from the nest. I watched closely, trying my best to see the nest and not plow it to oblivion. If I spotted it, I would raise the cultivator and carefully drive over or around the eggs. Sometimes, no matter how hard I watched, I failed to see the nest. The next round, the pair would meekly fly to the side as I passed the area, informing me that I had failed in my mission.

If I came upon a family in which the young had already hatched, one of the parents would fake its injury while the other led their long-legged offspring to safety. One day I discovered a nest with several newly-hatched babies. They couldn't have been more than an hour old; one was still wet from the moisture of the egg. I got off the tractor and attempted to chase them to the side. Three ran off, but two ran toward my tractor and hid far under the rubber tread of the back tire. I carefully dug them out and released them to the custody of their frantic parents. Little brown and white fluffballs on stilts.

Neighbors often worked in adjoining fields while I cultivated in ours. Some days we worked at opposite ends and never found ourselves in the same area at the same time. On others, you could tell well in advance that our progress would gradually bring us together. The first to reach the end of the field where our paths were about to meet would stop his tractor and wait. When the other arrived, we got off and met at the fence. We talked a short while and then returned to our tractors and to our jobs. The methods of power and transportation may have changed, but this relationship between farm neighbors has likely gone on for thousands of years.

I was even more tired than usual; the sun was hot and it had been a late night. A township road bordered the south end of the eighty. The opposite end, over a rolling hill, ended a half mile to the north, out of sight from the road and from our farm. I reached the far end and couldn't go on. I shut off the tractor, put my head on the steering wheel, and fell asleep. A half hour later I awoke and, somewhat refreshed, headed back down the field. I topped the hill and there, at the place I would arrive at the road, a car stood waiting.

It was a salesman. He had seen me go north over the hill and, thinking it was my father on the tractor, waited for his return. Disgusted with his long wait and with the identification of the driver, he asked in a gruff tone, "What took you so long?"

"I had to replace a broken shovel," I lied.

Each noon and at 5:30 in the afternoon, I would drive into our yard and shut the tractor off at our gas pump. Instead of quiet, the noise continued; for several minutes the sound of the engine continued to ring in my ears.

If asked if I think those long hours on the tractor are what damaged my hearing, I will likely respond: "What?"

Heart Attack

There aren't many things about growing up I would take back.

Dad never seemed to get sick and, except when he was recovering from back surgery, never missed work.

We were repairing a piece of machinery one morning when he calmly turned and said, "Wayne, you have to help me to the hospital. I think I am having a heart attack."

He recovered rapidly and was sent home with strict instructions to spend the next several days in bed.

Late one afternoon, I finished the chores and went up to his room. I rested next to him on my mom's side of the bed and began telling him how things were going outside. Dad reached over and placed his hand on my arm.

I recoiled. "What?"

Dad withdrew his hand and into himself. "I just wanted to touch you."

Our family wasn't good at showing affection.

I wish I could take that time back.

Vern's

Vern's Recreation Hall, a multi-leveled, multi-recreational establishment, was located on Main Street, across from the old Noonan Hotel. A dark, narrow, creaking wooden stairway, accessed from the sidewalk, led to the bowling alley on the upper floor, a fire marshal's nightmare.

The alley had three lanes, each served by a manual pinsetter. For me, the bowling alley was a source of both recreation and income. Financially, it was a break-even proposition. If I was allowed to go to town on a weekend afternoon, I would hurry up the steps hoping to get an opportunity to set pins. The establishment employed regular pinsetters for their weeknight leagues, but on Saturday and Sunday afternoons they relied on amateurs like myself. Pinsetters were paid ten cents a line and bowling cost thirty cents. The normal plan for young weekend setters was to set pins for three, or maybe six, lines and then move to the front of the alley and barter their earnings for bowling rights.

I don't believe that today the manual pinsetting machines would be OSHA approved. I perched high on a wide board behind and off to one side of the lane. The ball rolled though the pins, knocking those dislodged into the pit. I quickly jumped into the pit, picked up the ball, and sent it rolling back to the bowler along an elevated channel. I then picked up the felled pins and slid them into slots on the rack, making sure to finish the job and jump back on my perch before the bowler threw the ball back down the alley in an attempt to pick up his spare. I then repeated the procedure, returning the ball and putting the newly downed pins into the empty slots. Lastly, I pulled down on a metal bar that lowered the entire rack onto the floor and released the full rack of pins onto their spots.

The dangers of this profession were many; some bowlers seemed to consider pinsetters more as targets than as necessary assistants. The ball was sometimes thrown before the rack was raised, allowing the setter a split second to jump from the pit to his perch. Pins would sometimes spin into the gutter and come to rest several feet up the alley. This required crawling on one's belly under the rack and hoping to escape back into the pit before the next ball came flying down the alley.

The biggest danger came from the fireballers; to some bowlers, speed was more important than accuracy. A bowler of this ilk would take an amazingly high backswing and, with the ball lifted straight above his shoulder, throw with all his might. Pins would fly everywhere, up into the rack, high off the padded backboard, and occasionally into the next alley. There was a terrifying rumor that Bill Wilness, a six-foot-five local painter, once sent a pin flying through a high back window and onto the parking area behind the bowling alley. Volleys of swear words could sometimes be heard streaming from the pits after an exceptionally hard-thrown ball blasted through the pins.

My career as a pinsetter was short lived; when I was a sophomore, Clem Etter opened a modern bowling alley with automatic pinsetters and my skills became obsolete.

The lower half of Vern's establishment was a pool hall. I first saw the inside of Vern's when I was in elementary school. Snake dances were illegal. As part of Thursday night's pre-game homecoming celebration, students would gather on Main Street and hold hands, forming a chain of fifty to a hundred students. The front person would lead the participants twisting and turning through the downtown area. In this, my only experience with snake dancing, we were led into a back alley and through the back door of the pool hall. Back and forth we went, around each pool table and eventually out the front door. Vern's motley crew of interrupted customers eyed us with varying looks of surprise, amusement, and disgust. Little did I know this den of iniquity would one day become my second home.

I'm not sure if it was against the law for unescorted, underage youths to enter establishments that sold beer. If it was, Vern had made a conscious decision to ignore the law in exchange for monetary considerations. The same year the bowling alley closed, I moved my business downstairs to the pool hall.

One cement step up from Main Street aligned you with Vern's doorsill; the irresistible lure of sin carried you through. Your senses were flooded. The smell of stale beer and tobacco filled the air. Hank Williams twanged a lonesome ballad from the old Seeburg Jukebox to the right of the door and a brass-railed, cigarette-burned bar extended along the left. Regulars slouched on their barstools staring into amber glasses, oblivious to everything but the rising bubbles. One would occasionally turn and spit a dark stream of tobacco juice in the general direction of the closest spittoon.

Past Hank was a row of high-backed wooden booths where euchre players dealt two or three cards at a time from their thin decks. They bid and played their hand rapidly, as if they had somewhere else to be. Cards were slammed down in triumph and dimes grudgingly exchanged at the end of each game.

Green-felted tables filled the back half of the room. First came the large snooker table with its strange combination of red and numbered balls and its unbelievably small pockets. The billiard table was next; it had no pockets at all. What was that all about? The back of the hall held three standard pocket billiard tables, full-sized, not the miniature coin-operated tables found in bars today. Rows of cues secured in felt clamps lined one wall and wooden, button-like markers, slid back and forth to keep score, were strung on long overhead wires.

Players, most of whom were contributing to the thick haze of smoke that hung over the room, stalked the tables, grimly squinting along their cues. Balls cracked and recoiled, careening off the rubber, felt-covered cushions. This was serious business; although very few played for money, it was custom for the loser to pay for the game. Vern charged twenty-five cents for a game of snooker and ten cents for pocket billiards, which we simply called pool. Billiard players were charged by the minute. This was a moot point since that table was rarely used.

Vern, tall, bald-headed, and usually emotionless, ruled this motley assortment from atop a high backless stool near one corner of the bar. The education of a pool player was slow, humiliating and, in most cases, expensive. Learning to hold a cue properly was a slow process and making a ball in the correct pocket unlikely. I began my education playing eight-ball on the pool tables. Unless an opponent pocketed the cue ball by accident and automatically lost, I paid for nearly every game. The fact that a few of my opponents were only slightly more experienced than me was my only salvation.

There was usually a waiting list to get on the snooker table. I could never understand why Vern didn't invest in a second snooker table and replace the seldom-used billiard table. Snooker is a complicated game. If any numbered ball or the cue ball falls into an uncalled or incorrect pocket, it is a scratch and points are subtracted from your score. Vern lost money when my friends and I were learning to play. It took forever for us to complete those first games; sometimes one player or team, if we played partners, would win the game with a negative score.

Vern opened the pool hall at eight each morning and closed at midnight. Most of the time, especially at night when most of his business was at the pool tables, he dozed precariously on his stool. No one but Vern was allowed to rack the balls. When a game was completed, one of the players would bump the butt end of his cue twice on the wooden floor. Vern would open his eyes, climb down from his stool, collect his money, rack the balls, and return to his stool. Players learned never to cross Vern; if they tried to cheat by extending a game after it should have ended, he could sense it in his sleep and would explode in anger.

I began spending more and more time in the pool hall and gradually my skill level improved; by the time I graduated from high school I had abandoned the smaller tables and played only snooker.

Some of the most enjoyable and memorable times of my life were spent in the pool hall. Winter afternoons were the best. I was farming with Dad and we usually finished our outside work by noon. I would have the afternoon, until chore time, to hang out at Vern's. Most of the boys my age had gone off to college or had daytime jobs; this was the time farmers, men who had learned from the old masters but now seldom played, would come to town. They would enter the back door, stomp the snow off their feet, and stand near the table, watching. These men were quiet and calm, not cocky and driven like some younger players I could mention.

When asked if they wanted to play, they would hang up their coats and carefully select a cue from the rack. They moved around the table in their four-buckle boots and bib overalls as graceful as ballet dancers. The games with these gentlemen were the best. They understood the game; their shot selection and cue ball control was unlike anything I was used to seeing. They were far better players than I was, but because I played nearly every day and they only a few times a year, the games were usually competitive. Gracious in victory or defeat, these men showed me the true meaning of sportsmanship, a virtue that was easy to see and respect but difficult to adopt.

I remember one day in particular. Christmas vacation had brought many of my friends back to Madelia. Mom and Dad had gone on a short vacation, leaving me in charge of the farm. I got up early, finished all the chores in semi-darkness, and was waiting when Vern opened his front door at eight o'clock. I played snooker all morning with some of the locals and, by early afternoon, my friends began wandering in and joining our games. I rushed home at four to do the evening chores and was back at the hall before six. We played snooker until Vern chased us out at midnight. It had been a good day; I didn't lose a game in over fourteen hours of playing.

The second summer after I graduated from high school was a difficult one. I would hang out with friends, usually closing the pool hall, and then go to the Triangle Cafe for a late snack. The following morning I would be in the field early and cultivate corn until five o'clock. This routine was repeated day after day and, with each repetition, I became more and more tired. The day finally came, as the heat increased and the rows of corn became more and more blurry, that I decided I would have to make a change in my behavior. I resolved to go to bed immediately after supper, hoping a good twelve-hour sleep would help me recover from my exhaustion.

My after-supper thinking went something like this: "Nothing ever happens in Madelia." "What if something did happen and I missed it?" "I suppose it wouldn't hurt to go to town for an hour or so; I could still be in bed by eight."

Midnight would find me back in my booth at the Triangle, and the next day I would be even more exhausted. This time my resolution was absolute; there was no way I could survive another day like this. Supper. "I guess I could go to town for a few minutes, just to check out what's happening."

I was nineteen when I decided to get my military service out of the way and joined the MN National Guard. Fort Leonard Wood, Missouri, was a cold, dreary, godforsaken camp. Its only redeeming quality was its spectacular pool hall. Here was a place I could escape from structured military discipline. On the tables everyone was equal in rank.

I quickly learned I was a small fish in a large pond. Players played nine-ball, a game that might last two minutes, betting more than one of my day's wages with each game. A player would sometimes stand next to a table and hand over five dollar bills, not even getting a shot, as his opponent ran the table time after time. George Fels, a member of my basic training company, was one of the biggest gamblers. I remember that from time to time he would send home to Chicago for more cash. I was surprised when I recently googled George's name and found he has written several instructional books on pool.

There were no Hank Williams songs on Fort Leonard Wood's jukebox. The latest top ten hits were all I heard; unfortunately, I heard them to death. Groups of soldiers came and went throughout the day, each adding more coins but pushing the same buttons. I never hear "El Paso," "Running Bear," or Wilbert Harrison's "Kansas City" without thinking of those days in that big pool hall.

My friend Dave Erickson and I were born on the same day. Dave happened to be in town on the afternoon of our twenty-first birthdays. We decided to celebrate by having a beer in Vern's. We climbed up on tall stools and each placed fifteen cents on the bar. Vern came over smiling, thinking we were having fun with him. "You guys aren't twenty-one."

He carefully examined the IDs we handed him and, I think still a little skeptical, gave us each a glass of Grain Belt. As far as I remember, this was the first time Dave, who looked at least as young as me, had been in Vern's establishment. He didn't play pool. Vern had known me for years, but from observing my appearance and my behavior, had no reason to suspect that I was an adult.

This was the only beer I ever drank at Vern's. I think it entirely appropriate that here was where I chose to take my first legal drink.

I rarely play pool anymore; when I do, I'm disappointed. The skill I once maintained with constant practice is gone. Not so my admiration for the bib-overalled champions of my youth. That continues to grow.

New Year's Eve

The Ericksons had moved to Frazee, in northwestern Minnesota. Dave spent most of his college Christmas vacation with his parents but came down to Madelia for New Year's Eve. We drove around town in my new Chevy, wondering what we should do for excitement.

Dave had a new girlfriend in Frazee. She and some of her cute friends were going to a party at a nearby roadhouse. Wouldn't it be fun to show up and surprise them at midnight? It was nine o'clock and more than two hundred and thirty miles. Quick math showed we could make it if we averaged eighty miles an hour. Buoyed by the calculations, we acted. There was no time for delay.

Dave navigated. We only drove a hundred on the straighter sections.

Near Painesville, the land became hilly. Far behind, I saw headlights; every so often they flashed into view before being swallowed by the rolling terrain. They were definitely getting closer. I dropped to fifty-five and was amazed at how fast the gap closed.

The cop caught up with us as we entered the thirty-mile-an-hour zone, just as we were passing a busy nightclub. He slowed and signaled a turn. I held it at thirty. He pulled out of his faked turn and accelerated to within a few feet of my rear bumper. He rode there a few seconds, then, with adrenaline-induced anger and frustration, floored his big cruiser, fishtailed around us, and sped away.

There was little time for caution; it was going to be close. We pulled into the roadhouse a little before twelve thirty and hurried inside.

Dave's girlfriend was there with another guy. The discussion quickly escalated to a heated argument.

We climbed back into the Chevy and started home.

My teetotaling mom was sure she knew how we had spent New Year's Eve when we kept nodding off during the bowl games.

BIRDS

Feder is the German word for feather. Whether cultural or genetic, I have had an interest in and have kept birds of one kind or another for much of my life.

Dad was complicit. He grew up on a farm that swarmed with flocks of poultry and, while I don't remember, must have helped me with my earliest acquisitions.

Birds seemed to show up and come under my care. Care, in this case, was a nebulous concept; avian survival on our farm was more closely aligned with natural selection than with animal husbandry. Free range is certainly not a new concept. My poultry roamed and scavenged the farm for much of the year; it was only during the coldest months that they were rounded up and fed and watered in an old building behind the machine shed.

My flocks provided many a meal for hungry hawks and owls and for the mink and raccoons that wandered up from our sloughs. Fortunately mine was a "not-for-profit" enterprise. Except for a few eggs that were half-heartedly collected and the sacrifice of the occasional fat duck or chicken for the table, the goal was equilibrium.

Our farm was populated, off and on, with several breeds of meat-producing ducks, including Mallard-patterned Rouens, white Pecans, and Swedish Blues with a big white spot in the center of their breast. There were tall, upright Indian Runners and hissing Muscovy ducks, a breed that originated in Central America.

I got up early most fall mornings to hunt ducks on our sloughs. One morning I was thrilled to see a small flock of snow geese barely visible through a dense screen of fog. I crept as close as I dared, raised my shotgun, and fired. When all but two ran across the water instead of flying away like any self-respecting goose, I realized I had shot two of my tame white ducks.

I had a brief dalliance with Guinea Fowl, gray hunched-back critters that slept in trees, cackled incessantly, and refused to be tamed.

There were chickens of all sizes and colors. The conglomeration of types gradually diminished as the breeds hybridized with or were outcompeted by the hardy diminutive bantams.

You're probably wondering how to hypnotize a chicken. First, catch a chicken. Next, place it on the ground with its neck and beak fully extended. Take a finger (one of yours, not one of the chicken's) and slowly draw a foot-long line on the ground, forward from the tip of the bird's beak. Repeat fifteen times. Carefully release the bird and quietly walk away. The chicken will remain motionless in this ridiculous position for a minute or two before coming to its senses, self-consciously looking around, and casually strolling back to the flock.

Two individuals from this vast collection of chickens stand out in my mind.

My Aunt Florence in Hancock, Minnesota, owned a large, buff-colored rooster, one that I admired and I suppose coveted. One trip, as we were getting into the car for the drive home, Florence emerged her garage with a large, wiggling burlap sack. For at least one summer the big bird strutted through my flock as king of the farmyard.

I was nineteen; it was the winter before I began serving my six months of active duty in the National Guard. My long-neglected flock had dwindled down to a single bird: an ancient Old English Game Bantam. His survival was primarily due to his habit of roosting each night on our barn's manure carrier track, far above the reach of hungry predators. Perhaps this grizzled, long-spurred cock had been the dominant bird when he still had companions, but he now claimed that role unchallenged. My duty was to sow a small seed of doubt.

Evenings, as I worked in the barn doing chores, I would let loose my best imitation of a rooster's crow. The bantam would crow back. He would immediately respond whether I crowed ten times in rapid succession or if I waited several minutes between crows. He would answer if I crowed from the hayloft or from the pump shed. He returned my every call from the distant beef barn or from my pigeon loft. The last thing I would hear as I walked to the house through the early winter darkness was his final triumphant reply.

Pigeons were my biggest avian weakness. I captured six-week-old babies from the nooks and crannies of our barn from the time I was eight years old and, when I got older, devised ways of catching adult birds. My pigeons were kept in cages, crates, and unused buildings from which they usually found a way to escape. One day Dad told me if I would "get rid of those damned barn pigeons" he would help me find some domestic birds.

A few days later, he helped me build a real pigeon loft with a wire fly pen and, later that evening, we drove to Ed Lasses' farm a few miles west of us. I returned holding four beautiful pure-white pigeons in a cardboard box. A monster had been created.

Over the next several years, a parade of fancy breeds arrived at our train depot and passed through my lofts: tri-colored Modenas, English Trumpeters with large crests and feathered feet, Fantails with tails that spread like a peacock, and Pouters that inflated their balloon-like crops.

A 1957 cover story in *American Pigeon Journal* featured Russ Harter from Ohio, then-president of the United Roller Club of America. I wrote to Mr. Harter and asked if he would sell me some Rollers. Rollers spin backward during flight in a series of somersaults. Several long months later, a wooden crate containing twelve six-week-old rollers arrived at the depot. For a dollar a bird and three dollars shipping, I had found the perfect pigeon.

I have shown or flown rollers almost continuously for the last forty years in spite of being critically allergic to the dust produced by their feathers. As I write this short story in the summer of 2014, lofts on my farm hold more than a hundred and fifty Birmingham Rollers, a number I carefully attempt to conceal from Lynda.

Fooling Around

The fall I was nineteen I decided to join the National Guard and fulfill my military obligation. I wasn't necessarily expecting Uncle Sam to make a man out of me, but I did assume that basic training would be strenuous and challenging. I had a couple months to get ready, so I did daily pull-ups on our manure carrier track and sit-ups and push-ups in the evenings while I watched TV.

Three weeks before Christmas, Richard Ellingsberg and I joined a group in Minneapolis and took the long train ride to Fort Leonard Wood, Missouri. My recollections of the first few weeks of basic training are mostly of standing in lines or marching around on the streets of our base. Our cross section of American youth turned out to be a disappointing crew. Many made Gomer Pyle appear to be a worldly genius. Others, college kids from Chicago, were brash and loudmouthed, unlike anyone I had ever met. I was surprised to find that even the most soft and nonathletic of these city dwellers, used to walking city streets, could march for miles without seeming to tire, but would drop out of formation after a block or two of easy jogging.

Our training battalion was composed of ten companies, each with about a hundred men. Half of the men were in National Guard units and the remainder, regular Army enlistees. I was in Bravo Company. Who could fail to be inspired?

Early in the second week of training it was announced that we were going to participate in a physical fitness test. I now knew how Tom felt when he battled Captain Najork and his hired sportsmen. All the things I had learned while fooling around were suddenly put in play. We did burpees, a strange contortion of dropping to a push-up position and then back to our feet. There were pull ups, push ups, sit ups, and a three-hundred-yard run. War was obviously much like monkey bars, tackle tag, track and field, and climbing into cupolas. We were timed in the three hundred and given thirty seconds to perform as many as we could of each of the other four activities.

A few days later, Sergeant Ferrar, our Bravo Company sergeant, called me aside and told me that mine was the highest score in the battalion.

Fame and fitness are fleeting. We returned home for Christmas, then back for more standing in line, marching, calisthenics, target practice, and winter survival camping. The last week of basic training we were given a second fitness test, one calculated to demonstrate the fruits of our efforts. As we left for the fitness training area, our sergeants, in order to impress their superiors, encouraged us to embellish our scores.

I tried my best but refused to cheat. My score was considerably lower than when I began my training.

The army made a mistake by not hiring me to teach their recruits a class in fooling around.

4-H

Before every meeting we would recite the 4-H pledge: "I pledge my head to clearer thinking, my heart to greater loyalty, my hands to larger service, and my health to better living, for my club, my community, my country, and (added since my time in 4-H) my world." Some members in the 1950s failed to meet or even strive to reach these lofty goals. They were only in 4-H to show livestock.

I grew up during the heyday of the South St. Paul's Union Stockyards, a time when this company was one of the two or three largest livestock marketers in the world. Large packers like Armour and Swift operated twenty-four hours a day and hired thousands of workers, slaughtering millions of cattle, sheep, and hogs each year.

The Union Stockyards and the packing companies decided in the 1930s to use their extensive resources to sponsor a livestock show for Minnesota 4-H members. The Junior Livestock Show quickly became one of the leading shows in the nation, rivaling the International Livestock Show in Chicago and the prestigious shows in Denver, Kansas City, and Fort Worth.

The goal of any 4-H member who competed with beef cattle, sheep, or hogs was to place high enough in their county fair to advance to the Junior Livestock Show and, once there, place high enough again to qualify for the end-of-show auction. Large companies purchased the auction animals to advertise and promote their businesses. The top animals might receive several times their normal market value.

I showed beef steers for six years, from the time I was sixteen until I was twenty-one. Showing became a passion with me; it was one of the primary reasons I remained home on the farm as long as I did. Kids who went to college could only show until they were nineteen; if they were away at school, their father would be taking care of their animals and not the 4-H member.

Each October, the Sumption brothers shipped two hundred fancy shorthorn steer calves from their ranch in northern South Dakota to the sale barn in Worthington, Minnesota.

We left home early on Saturday morning and arrived at the sale barn around nine. The alleys were packed with buyers and the pens filled with beautiful, high-quality club calves. Sumption's calves had a great reputation and buyers came from many states. Not only had they produced several Junior Livestock Show Champions, but their steers had also placed high at the other big shows around the country.

Showing beef steers is similar to most kinds of competition: the skill and interest level of the participants range from casual to obsessive. It wasn't an easy activity. Parents were usually deeply involved; in many cases they fed beef cattle on their farms and had the knowledge and facilities to help make their son's or daughter's project a success.

My brother Arlo and I were fortunate. Dad liked cattle and was willing to help us buy our calves and provide the feed and equipment we needed to do well.

We weren't in the elite group competing against each other to buy the top calves at Sumption's sale. Some of the customers were there to buy only the best; they had traveled to Sumption's ranch and studied the calves in the pasture. They knew which cows and cow lines had a record of producing winners and which bulls were the outstanding sires. It took money and effort to win at the big shows. Some of these competitors enhanced their chance of winning by purchasing two or three high-priced calves from near the top of the sale order.

Many of the best calves were in the first pens, closest to the barn. We didn't spend much time looking at these; they were out of our price range. We studied the calves farther down the alley, hoping to find a gem, or at least a likely prospect, from the younger or more poorly conditioned animals. When I found a calf I liked, I would talk about it with Dad and, if he agreed with my assessment, write its ear-tag number on a blank page in our sale catalog. I would eventually compile a list of five or six calves that I hoped would fall into my price range.

The sale was ready to start. We hurried inside and found a place in the crowded arena. I almost held my breath as the first lot was released into the sale ring. A beautifully groomed long-haired calf walked out into the deep sawdust floor and one of the ring men chased it slowly around the arena. Pairs or small clusters of buyers would lean together and whisper, glancing back and forth between their group and the calf.

The auctioneer, after introducing the Sumption brothers and issuing a short statement extolling the high quality of their cattle, would open the sale. He was old and wore a white, narrow-brimmed western-style hat. His chant was quiet and hypnotic. "Want im at three, want im at three, want im at three, now ya go four, now ya go four." The volume and the speed of his chant would gradually increase with the price of the calf. Bang! The gavel fell and the calf was sold for somewhere near five hundred dollars. New cars sold for less than two thousand.

This was neither the Sumption brothers' nor the auctioneer's first rodeo. Human psychology was being applied at every turn. The time spent on selling each calf was carefully planned. A higher price might be obtained if the auctioneer worked hard and long on a single lot, but this would slow the sale and drag down the enthusiasm. They wanted to keep the excitement at a fever pitch and buyers quickly learned to "bid or get off the pot."

The best calves were placed in the top third of the sale order but were not necessarily among the first few sold. The goal was to keep the prices as high as possible by interspersing a really good calf into the lineup from time to time while still making sure they sold before the big buyers ran low on cash.

A beautiful roan March calf entered the ring. A hush passed over the crowd as everyone turned to look. The usual whispers elevated to a soft buzz; this was the one they had been waiting for. The auctioneer wasn't in a rush to sell this one. A sale topper of this quality would be talked about and written up in cattle journals across the country. The calf was sold to a Minnesota buyer and I knew I would be seeing it again when the big fall show arrived.

I squeezed my sale number and watched as the first calf on my list entered the ring. Dad always let us bid on our own calves. I don't think he ever told us how much was too much but we could feel when that point had been reached. The price quickly passed my limit; I didn't even bother to bid. The calves I wanted didn't come into the ring in the order I had them ranked on my list, so it was hard to decide if I should pass up an affordable calf now and hope that the one I really wanted didn't go too high later on.

Arlo and I would each eventually buy a calf we liked. Dad would write out the check and we would assist the yardmen as they drove our calves up the chute and into the back of our pickup. We were excited all the way home, sure our new purchases would turn out to be champions.

Dad's cattle were kept in the cement feedlot and the big barn. Our club calves were pampered, kept in a long, straw-bedded pen in the little barn. We watched them carefully the first few days to make sure they didn't catch shipping fever from the stresses of weaning and travel, and then gradually began increasing the quality and quantity of their feed. In a few weeks they were thriving on a full feed of ground corn, soybean concentrate, and alfalfa hay.

It was nine months until the county fair. My calf gradually calmed down; soon I could walk in the pen without alarming him and scratch his back while he ate. One day I slipped a leather halter over his head and buckled it in place. It was time to teach him to lead. I snapped a lead rope to a ring on the bottom of his halter, tied the end of the rope to a metal stanchion pipe, and let him struggle. Some calves quieted down and stopped fighting the rope on the first day; wilder ones required several hour-long sessions before they realized they were not being harmed and could not escape.

The calf was no longer afraid of me or of being tied; teaching him to lead would now be a simple matter. I held the rope firmly and pulled his head to one side. He turned to face me to relieve the pressure. I let him stand quietly a short time and then repeated the maneuver. He quickly learned to turn with me as I circled around him. The same strategy was then applied with straight-ahead pressure and the calf was soon following me around the pen.

Winter finally ended. We opened the door and turned the calves into the small fenced lot on the north end of the barn. They would buck and run and play, then calm down and quietly investigate every corner of their new world. It was fun to come out in the evening and walk in the yard with them and scratch their backs, or stand back and try to assess their progress and potential.

School ended and it was time to introduce the calves to the world outside their small lot. We led them around our farmyard for a few evenings and then began taking them for long walks down our gravel road. The outings helped them become calm, confident, and fit. A good show steer had to be fat but it also had to have good muscle tone and show no fear in the show ring.

The summer warmed, and our thoughts and plans turned more and more toward the fair. We switched on the big fan that blew lengthwise down the long pen and locked the calves in during the day. The windows were darkened, and every few hours we soaked the calves with a fine mist. We were growing hair. Their wet coat was brushed upward and allowed to dry in front of the cooling fan; a coat of long, shiny hair would hide flaws and be sure to attract the judge's attention. Hair made a good calf better.

We soaked, shampooed, and rinsed our calves. We trimmed their feet and clipped the hair on their faces and upper tail. The fancy leather show halters were brought out of storage and cleaned and polished.

It was entry day. Big Pete, our local trucker, sent one of his smaller straight trucks to pick up our calves. We led them up the rickety chute and tied the end of their rope halters to metal rings along one wall of the truck. Dad had the pickup ready, and we jumped in and headed for St. James. We wanted to get there ahead of the calves.

Six years. Six fairs. Many of the details have faded and blended together. I do remember that there were three days to fool around and one to be deadly serious.

The show order was posted on a big sheet of paper taped to the wall of the old clay block cattle barn. I knew how long it took to wash, brush, and dry my steer. I put on presentable clothes, picked up the show stick that I used to position my calf's feet, and led him through a narrow alley into the show arena.

The Shorthorn class was small; I had a good chance to win that division. When first place in the Angus and Herford classes had also been selected, the three winners were brought into the ring and lined up. The judge walked around each animal, studying it carefully one last time. He ran his hands over their backs and along their ribs to check their conditioning and then requested that their owners lead them around the ring in a large circle so he could watch the way they walked and make his final comparisons.

The steers were stopped near the center of the arena, and the judge walked slowly down the line. He stopped, raised his hand, and slapped one of the steers loudly on the rump, the time-honored method of declaring the champion. The audience applauded, some members more loudly than others; a few frowns and harsh whispers revealed that not everyone agreed with the judge's decision.

We weren't done yet. Each county was allotted a certain number of steers to represent our county at the Junior Livestock Show, usually six from Watonwan County. The top six animals in each division were led back into the arena and lined up in the order they had placed. The first place Angus, Herford, and Shorthorn was brought forward and the judge picked the first calf that would advance to St. Paul. As far as I know this was always the champion. The steer that had placed second in the champion's division was brought forward to join the remaining two and the judge selected our number two representative. As each additional steer was selected, the steer behind him was brought forward so the judge always had three animals to choose from. I remember feeling the tension build as we neared the county's quota and my calf had not yet been selected to advance.

The champion female beef animal was brought into the arena following the selection of the champion steer, and the Junior Livestock Show lineup and the grand champion beef animal was selected between the champion steer and champion female.

The last beef event was the showmanship competition. This contest was perhaps the most fair because you didn't need a high-powered or high-quality calf to be competitive. Throughout the day, the judge observed which competitors were doing the best job presenting their animals and would ask him or her to return for the showmanship division. The winner was selected for their ability to groom, lead, and present their animal according to the latest show and etiquette guidelines.

I went down to my basement recently and dug through an old box of 4-H mementos. I found two grand champion ribbons and others that read champion. I do remember I won the showmanship division several times; it was my favorite. I also found show catalogs for five of the six Junior Livestock Shows I attended. I had forgotten that one year I didn't qualify with my steer but was lucky enough to win the county fair with a Hampshire lamb I had raised and was able to show it instead.

1961 was my last year in 4-H and one I will never forget. I had three excellent steers that year: an Angus, a Herford, and a Shorthorn. Only two could be shown at the county fair, so I had to leave my Angus home.

It's fun to remember how I came to possess my Shorthorn calf. It was late in the Sumption sale, and I had already purchased a calf. I had been looking at a small, dark roan calf earlier in the pens but couldn't decide if he was good enough to buy as a second calf. The calves entered the ring through a narrow chute where a helper quickly brushed up their sides and hindquarters before releasing them into the ring. I knew the calf was up next so I walked down to the chute to have one last look. I noticed the worker was a man whose children had won two grand championships at the Junior Livestock Show. He brushed the calf's hair up as he normally did, but just before it was released into the arena, he combed the hair down flat.

He knew something about the calf that I didn't. He started to bid, thinking he could buy it at a low price so late in the sale. I stood behind him. Each time he bid, I waited a few seconds and then held up my auction number and raised the bid. He soon realized he was not going to get the calf at a bargain price and gave up. He looked disgustedly around the arena, trying to see who had been bidding against him.

The little calf continued to grow and get better and better. By early summer I could tell he was going to be special. I had never worked harder with a calf; his hair was long and silky and he was perfectly trained. He placed first at the fair and my Herford second.

I had high hopes for the Junior Livestock Show. I thought I could place near the top of my class and might also have a chance to win the showmanship award; I had placed third two years earlier with a calf that had not been as well trained.

The morning of the show I was washing my calf as I usually did when he began to bawl. I don't know what caused him to become upset, but he wouldn't quit. He bawled while I groomed him and when I led him into the ring. He bawled the whole time he was being judged. All my hopes of being called out for the showmanship contest were dashed.

The Shorthorns were separated into two divisions; the lightweight class had over thirty entrants. My calf was in first place for much of the judging but at the last minute was switched to second place. I never imagined I would place so high. The top two in each class were brought back to the arena for the selection of the grand and reserve champions of the show, and I got to watch the final placings from the best seat in the house. My calf bawled his approval.

This was a good year for Arlo as well. He had a nice Angus calf that he had purchased from our neighbor, John Snyder. The calf was slow to develop and barely qualified for the Junior Livestock Show, but after the county fair it improved rapidly. He placed high in a large class and also qualified for the auction.

The auction took place the morning after the judging was completed. Seventy out of well over three hundred calves had qualified. My calf was scheduled to enter the ring in the top fifteen. I groomed and led him into the ring for the last time. Central Livestock, my father's selling agent at the Union Stockyards, purchased my steer and I received well over double its market value.

I led my calf out of the arena and into the alley along the side of the show barn where the Central photographer took a picture for their newsletter. I hope it was socially acceptable for a young man my age to choke up as his favorite animal in the world was led away.

Picking Corn

This story isn't about picking corn. Dad bought a new mounted corn picker for our DC Case tractor and announced that it would be my job to run and maintain the new machine. I'm sure, without directly saying so, he was telling me it was time I began acting more responsibly.

I don't believe I had ever made a decision to become a farmer; on the other hand, I had never made a decision not to become one. I guess I had never made a decision to become anything. High school had certainly not prepared me for any specific future. My classmates took difficult electives; I took the easiest classes available. Other students toiled at homework, studied for tests, and turned in assignments. I read library books during class, clowned around, and hoped to absorb enough information to pass my tests. I suppose my friends had plans for the future but I don't recall the subject ever coming up. School ended and I drifted into farming, where my father, although we never actually discussed it, always expected me to be.

I worked hard enough on the farm but never became fully engaged. There must have been a big picture, but I couldn't see or feel it and found no reason to set goals or think about what the future might hold.

When Dad was a young boy, his father had given him a checkbook and allowed him to write checks for whatever he needed. Dad did the same for me, but somehow the arrangement never felt right; it was as if everything belonged to my father and I was just along for the ride. I didn't understand why I felt the way I did or know what to do about it. I slowly became more and more unhappy.

One day I was picking corn and a large flock of geese circled, set their wings, and landed in the field next to ours. It suddenly occurred to me that hunting, one of my great passions and a daily fall activity since the sixth grade, had come to an end. Farmers didn't chase geese on a whim. They grew up. They picked corn for weeks on end and, when that task was finished, plowed for many more weeks until the ground froze solid. They planted, cultivated, hayed, and harvested, all honorable endeavors. That day, sitting on the tractor seat with the geese drifting into the corn stubble, I decided I couldn't become a farmer.

Early that winter, Dad and I were working in the barn. I finally summoned the courage to tell him I wanted to go to college. It was difficult and I was afraid. I didn't really know if college was right for me, and I didn't want to disappoint my father.

Dad was crushed; he never doubted I would stay home and farm with him. He tried to talk me into staying.

A few days later I drove to Mankato and joined a milling mass of students in the college gymnasium. Bewildered and unsure, I moved from long line to long line, struggling to complete a class schedule from the mostly filled options.

I rarely hunted again after I left the farm. Years later, I took early retirement from high school teaching and became a farmer. I found satisfaction and fulfillment working unbelievably long hours planting, weeding, harvesting, cleaning, and marketing prairie seeds.

It was almost as if I had grown up.

Afterwards

A few years ago, I decided to write about some of the fun and crazy things I did when I was a kid. I sat at my computer and brainstormed, eventually coming up with about ten ideas. I started writing, plugging away in my slow, deliberate style. I crossed off each story as it was completed but would suddenly think of another adventure and add it to the bottom. The time has finally come, as Dad would say, "to stop this damn foolishness." As I look at my list, I see I have managed to whittle it down to about ten.

These little vignettes are wonderful and remarkable. Certainly not because of the way they are written or because of the antics they tell about one small boy. It is their magnification of the privilege and surroundings in which I grew up that gives them significance.

I still find it difficult to accept that while I played and wandered through a life of protection and innocence, surrounded by friends and family, much of the world lay in ruin. Nearly fifty million people died during the terrible war of my childhood and twenty million more were displaced afterwards, wandering through Europe and Asia, desperately attempting to return to their destroyed homes.

Thomas Wolfe wrote a book, published in 1940, the year of my birth, entitled "You Can't Go Home Again." The context of this highly acclaimed novel may not relate to my situation, but the title rings true.

A road trip around my hometown and surrounding countryside reveals a past shattered. Gone are the sloughs, drained while I was in college. Our farmstead appears empty and barren, its barns and silos bulldozed and burned by new owners. Wilson's Woods has been converted to farmland and a straggly tree plantation. Vern's, Adolf's, Ad's, and the old Noonan Hotel are all gone. Flanders Park, missing its log cabin, cannon, and bandstand, seems strangely small and sterile.

I stop sometimes, in my car or in my mind, and look around. I see a small boy running, climbing, and trying to keep one step ahead of trouble and marvel that he survived to become an old man.

Made in the USA
San Bernardino, CA
26 May 2015